ON DEADLINE
Managing Media Relations

Carole Howard

Wilma Mathews

WAVELAND
PRESS, INC.

Prospect Heights, Illinois

For information about this book, write or call:

Waveland Press, Inc.
P.O. Box 400
Prospect Heights, Illinois 60070
(708) 634-0081

CONTENTS

Carole Howard is vice president of public relations and communications policy at Reader's Digest, Pleasantville, New York, responsible for domestic and international public relations planning, media relations, corporate advertising, marketing promotions, employee communications and speechwriting. A former reporter, she worked for AT&T in Seattle and New York for 18 years in various public relations and marketing positions. She is a contributing author of Communicators' Guide to Marketing *and* Experts in Action: Inside Public Relations *(2nd edition), contributing editor of* Public Relations Quarterly *and a frequent speaker to public relations organizations and student groups. An accredited member of the Public Relations Society of America, Mrs. Howard is a current member of Women in Communications, Inc. and the International Association of Business Communicators, and a past member of National Press Women. She is listed in the Who's Who in America, Who's Who in the World and the International Directory of Distinguished Leadership.*

Wilma Mathews is a manager of public relations for AT&T. She has almost 20 years' experience with both profit and nonprofit organization. An accredited member of the International Association of Business Communicators (IABC), she has been a board member of that association and currently is chairman of the IABC Foundation. Ms. Mathews has spoken before numerous professional, civic and academic organizations and is a lecturer at the School of Visual Arts in New York. She is a contributor to Inside Organizational Communications, *2nd edition, and* Communicator's Guide to Marketing *and has written articles for several leading public relations journals. Ms. Mathews is a board member of the Council of Communication Management and is listed in the Who's Who of American Women and the International Who's Who of Women.*

FOREWORD

After all the research has been done and the organization has set its policies; after the news releases have been written; after management has approved them and the lawyers have cleared them, there remains the "small" task of distributing them to the news media.

If the news release has been soundly conceived and professionally prepared, chances are reasonably good that editors will accept it for publication in one form or another. But alas for all of us in public relations, a large percentage, perhaps even a majority, of media contacts will be handled poorly. Milliseconds after news releases have been opened, editors will deposit them in the "Big Round File." For the most part, they will concern events, or include information, of no interest to the medium receiving them. Not merely news releases, but any form of media contact—phone call, hand-written note, or whatever—will provide no return on the investment if it conveys the wrong message, or has been sent to the wrong medium, or to the wrong person at the right medium, or has been sent in the wrong format or at the wrong time. Wasted effort, wasted time, wasted money. No wonder, therefore, that editors who screen such material form a low opinion of public relations and its practitioners. News releases may be only the tip of the iceberg of media relations as some believe, but certainly as professionals we deserve to be judged by how well or poorly we perform this essential function.

All too often one hears that media relations isn't really public relations; it's "merely" publicity. Carole Howard and Wilma Mathews explain why media relations, properly practiced, must be preceded by policy determination, issue analysis, counseling and the like. They demonstrate convincingly that solid planning skills are necessary to practice successful media relations.

By limiting this book to the subject of media relations and enlarging the definition of this function, the authors restore media relations to its proper position. For this, they deserve the thanks of all of us in the profession. Both Mrs. Howard and Mrs. Mathews have worked in media relations for many years; their individual experience equals that of some entire corporate departments. There are few types of difficult situations they haven't already coped with successfully. You can be certain that their recommendations are based on experience in the "real world."

On Deadline is virtually an encyclopedia of media relations. Without stint or reserve, the authors share herein the breadth and depth of their experience. This book will provide much help to those who must "meet the press" (or interviewers from television, radio, or magazines). Whether you are responsible for calling an editor, or plan on managing a full media relations program, you will discover that Mrs. Howard and Mrs. Mathews have provided you with sound counsel.

Chester Burger
Chester Burger & Company, Inc.
New York, New York

PREFACE

We were in the midst of training a new person who had transferred into our media relations group when, about the same time, a colleague spoke over lunch of a similar situation at his company. "He's pestering all of us for hints on how to do his job," our friend said. "Why isn't there some book I can give him to read?"

"It sure would have been nice if someone had written it all down for us," we joked. And then, "One of us really ought to write that book." But even two robins do not make a spring. The conversation veered off in another direction, and writing the book became a dormant topic.

Shortly thereafter we responded to a late-night query from the *Wall Street Journal* after the leak of a layoff announcement. We had to coordinate responses to internal and external queries with spokespersons in twenty locations across the country. At one point a public relations manager in a manufacturing plant remarked, "You really ought to write this up—it would make a perfect case history."

Some time later we cancelled plans for a dinner together, one to write a speech on corporate media relations to a Public Relations Society of America chapter in Louisiana, the other to plan a workshop on media relations at the International Association of

Business Communicators annual convention in Chicago. At each of these functions we heard similar comments from members of the audience: "You have had so many different experiences with the news media you really ought to write a book." Thus, the idea came to life again. The fundamental tools of our trade are words. How flattering—and how humbling—to be told there is a need to sit down at your typewriter and bang out the story of how you spend your working life.

Education and training, even of a very high magnitude, are not enough. You also need experience. As cosmetics tycoon Helena Rubinstein put it, "First you've got to get educated—and then you've got to get smart." Our approach in this book will be to cite anecdotes and case histories from our combined three decades as public relations practitioners in the corporate and nonprofit worlds, and from the experiences of others who have graciously shared their stories with us. We hope you will find in them a freshness of vision that will enrich your own insights. Our goal is to provide direction, not directives. We will talk about the media relations job from both a strategic and a tactical point of view. And we will temper our advice with knowledge gained from our days as working reporters.

On Deadline begins with a discussion of the critical first step of planning a media relations program. There is nothing so wasteful of our resources or our energies than activity without insight. We also include a detailed description of setting goals and measuring results, for only with such operational systems in place will you be treated as equal members of the business team by others in your organization. We will offer tips on how to get your management's appproval *before* you begin and keep them informed of your progress and any changes in external or internal conditions as you proceed, so that your contributions are appreciated by the decision makers of the organization.

Architect Mies van der Rohe once said, "God is in the details" —and this is no less true of our profession than it was of his. With that in mind we offer specific suggestions on how to improve your relationship with reporters—including hints for ensuring that reporters can reach you at night, keeping your news release distribution lists up to date, creating interest in your organization with background mailings, deciding whether to announce your news in the morning or the afternoon, modifying your office coverage to match the media's hours, getting the most mileage out of clipping services, and deciding when to be responsive and when to say no. We also provide detailed instructions on how to background both your organization's spokesperson and the reporter before a major interview, because the preparation you put in before their meeting often makes the difference between success and failure. We will guide you in becoming a part of the decision–making process within your organization. You can take advantage of the instantaneous public opinion polls you can get from your ongoing contacts with reporters to counsel your organization's officers and board before practices and policies are set.

We have written *On Deadline* for a broad audience. Students of journalism and public relations should find insight into their fields no matter to which side of the profession they choose to devote their lives. Chief executive officers and other key spokespersons for organizations may find that parts of the book offer valuable background on how the media operate, and *On Deadline* may be useful as a handy reference before a reporter comes in for an inteview. Perhaps even reporters will find it interesting to glimpse the inner workings of the world of media relations. It may make them understand why we practitioners view ourselves—when we are doing our job well—as performing a valuable service that makes us not a barrier to information but rather indispensable translators of the needs of both reporters and our organizations.

Most of all, *On Deadline* is written for those people who are, or plan to be, responsible for an organization's or client's day-to-day relations with the news media. Whether you work for a bank wanting to publicize expanded financial services, a utility facing hostile reporters at a public hearing on a rate increase request, a social service agency desiring to generate attendance at a new job-counseling clinic, a trade association lobbying for legislation, or a large corporation marketing a new product, the media's coverage—or lack of coverage—of your news will be an important factor in the results.

A natural avenue into the world of public and media relations is to join a company or organization after a few years of experience as a reporter. For those of you who fell victim to the siren's song of journalism, the transition should not be difficult. Dealing with the media from this side can be just as stimulating as chasing after a story and a byline—indeed, we would argue more so, because you now have the opportunity to influence decisions and activities rather than just report them. You will have the same almost instant feedback as the media covers your organization's news on that evening's newscast, in tomorrow morning's newspaper or in the next issue of a magazine.

On the other hand, for people who have not spent time as reporters, producers, or editors, a move into the media relations position can be an abrupt change, requiring flexibility not only in *your* lifestyle but also in your family's as you strive to adapt to the media's sense of urgency. The workday's planned activities are forsaken when a reporter asks for information on your agency's fundraising expenses and it takes you several hours to gather the facts, arrange an interview and brief a spokesperson. A dinner party is interrupted when you receive word that there has been an accident at the plant and reporters are clamoring for information. A weekend outing is cancelled when you must move up your planned news conference by a week because of a change in the schedule of your organization's top officer. A night's sleep is lost when the clock is stopped during union bargaining as your organization works to negotiate a contract and avoid a walkout.

If you like order and predictability, and prefer to take a great deal of time to enunciate your views orally or in writing, media relations is not the job for you. But if you are stimulated by being at the center of action, enjoy responding to stimuli from several directions at once, can rapidly formulate thoughts and clearly articulate positions, find it exhilarating to bring definition to ambiguity, then media relations may be the field for you. Your energy and your ability to learn will be tested. The job requires people who can remain calm and focused in a crisis—and above all, keep their sense of humor and perspective. Your reward comes from the people you meet and the events you influence.

As the world has become more complex, business journalism has changed. It used to be relegated to the back pages of newspapers or to filling air time only on slow news days. Then creative financing of home mortgages, significant advances in research, dramatic corporate acquisitions, the popularity of personal computers and better educated customers put economics, finance, technology and business subjects onto the front pages. In newsrooms throughout the country additional reporters are being assigned to cover the economy. More pages are included in business sections. More air time is devoted to financial events. Economic issues have become personal issues—and thus news. Those of us who make our living by helping reporters translate such news into terms the general public can understand often feel as if we are living in an enormous clothesdryer—events are tumbling around us and we around them in a frantic, haphazard way. It is, after all, somewhat scary to see the words you spoke yesterday to a reporter on the phone set in type in this morning's *Seattle Post-Intelligencer* or *New York Times*.

At the same time, technology is revolutionizing the means by which we send and receive news, and challenging the traditional roles of print and broadcast media. Our home television set is being rapidly transformed into a new information tool as cable companies proliferate and teletext and videotex systems are introduced. Round-the-clock headline services and expanded television news programs are already here. In time, the merging computer and communications technologies will bring the "electronic newspaper" into our home via the television screen or another multifunctional terminal. The use of complex information management technologies is now a normal part of growing up. Our children's early exposure to computers as both learning tools and playthings means they are already trained to receive, generate and interact with text and graphics on a TV screen. Increasingly sophisticated communications networks allow the media to speed news via satellite and lightwave systems around the country, across borders and over oceans. A live video "feed" from the other side of the world is seen in true-to-life color and real time many thousands of miles away. Truly, the Information Age is here. We are only beginning to realize its opportunities and benefits for the exchange of information and news. In fact, possible applications are limited only by the imagination of the users of these technologies and of those who would serve us with interconnected networks, sophisticated terminals, expanded data bases and software programs.

It is easy to believe that with all the things competing for our time—particularly the growth and diversity of leisure activities—that people today are spending less time with newspapers, magazines, radio and television. But Alvin Toffler has observed: "For the more diverse the civilization—the more differentiated its technology, energy forms, and people—the more information must

flow between its constituent parts if the entirety is to hold
together, particularly under the stress of high change."[1] A recent
study by Barbara Bryant of Market Opinion Research in Detroit
showed that the proportion of time spent on mass media of various
forms has remained remarkably constant at 4% or 5% during the
last 50 years.

What has changed drastically, however, is the media mix and
the variety of offerings. Bryant's research shows that in the last 10
years people increased the time they spent viewing TV by 4 to 6
hours a week—at the expense of about an hour of reading time.
People are using media more and more as a secondary way to
spend time. They listen to the radio while driving, watch TV while
doing housework, scan newspapers and magazines during commercials on TV. There is much more scanning and gulping of information in and around other activities. There also are more special
interest publications catering to particular information needs and
interests.[2]

The public's thirst for information never seems to be quen-
ched. As Dan Rather opined: "In a world where it seems we're
inundated with news, I think we're only inundated with . . . well,
mutations of the news, imitations of the news, variations on the
news. When it comes to real and serious and important reportage
we're not glutted. We're starved."[3] And Robert MacNeil wrote in
his autobiography: "In most of the stories television cares to cover,
there is always 'the right bit,' the most violent, the most bloody,
the most pathetic, the most tragic, the most wonderful, the most
awful moment. Getting the effective 'bit' is what television news is
all about...."[4]

The public is demanding more of the news media, not only in
amount and variety but also in content. Accuracy. Sensitivity. And
yes, honesty. The editing process is an incredibly powerful tool,
carrying with it a great responsibility. Occasionally the obligation is
not met. Reporter Janet Cooke's fictitious tale of an eight-year-old
heroin addict named "Jimmy" was selected for the 1981 Pulitzer
prize; the story's subsequent repudiation by the *Washington Post*
brought dishonor on the newspaper that had once been hailed for
its Watergate revelations.[5] CBS News' television documentary,
"The Uncounted Enemy: A Vietnam Deception," aired in January
1982, was criticized severely by both General William C. West-
moreland and *TV Guide*. The criticism resulted in an internal

investigation at CBS (essentially acknowledging the accuracy of complaints on interviewing and editing techniques the network used in the program) and a well-publicized libel suit.[6] Such incidents bring dishonor not only to the reporters and editors involved but also, by association, to all journalists.

Similarly, misdeeds within the corporate and nonprofit worlds can foster distrust of all businesses and organizations. A charity charged with unnecessarily high administrative expenses, a company accused of knowingly marketing an unsafe product, a meat packer fined for fraudulently upgrading beef, a top government official disgraced by exposure of extravagantly padded expenses, and corporate executives convicted of illegal bribes to secure foreign sales—all these acts serve to reinforce biases and further stereotypes, not to mention that they prompt shareowners and customers to demand investigations and a full accounting. Clearly, the days are long gone when top officers of a company or organization could merely shrug off complaints with an irresponsible "the public be damned" attitude.

Demands on the people responsible for relations with the news media are also increasing. If we have not changed with the requirements of the job, then we have no doubt lost opportunities to serve our organizations, clients and profession. As Will Rogers put it, "Even if you are on the right track you will get run over if you just sit there."[7]

It was not all that many years ago when the press job in an organization was a seat-of-the-pants, responsive-type position. All we had to do was keep up friendships with reporters at local press association functions, keep our sense of humor when they phoned with tough questions, and keep the company's name out of the newspapers. Many corporations and organizations believed their decisions and actions were none of the media's—or the public's—business.

Today that has changed. For one thing, the name of our job has changed. It is *media* relations now, reflecting the ever increasing importance of television and radio as sources of news. For another thing, today's management expects more of us: Not only must we be able to get the organization *out* of a mess, but we also are expected to *keep it from ever getting into the mess in the first place*. Media relations people, like all public relations professionals, are moving rapidly into the more complex—and more ambiguous—world of issues and issues management. Not that we have moved out of the fire-fighting, news-releasing, question-answering business. That will be as important a part of what we do tomorrow as it is today. But it will not be the major thing we do, and it cannot be the only thing we let consume our time. It is no longer enough that we be good communicators with a wide knowledge of our organization and its product line. Now we must be familiar with everything from equal-opportunity laws to environmental-protection legislation, from workman's compensation to antitrust actions, from foreign competition to political action committees. In short, our skills and our work are expected to make a positive, measurable contribution to the organization's goals.

Good media relations requires thoughtful plans and targeted strategies. It is much more than churning out news releases on new products. It is searching for other opportunities and news events that can be turned into positive media coverage. It is taking time to develop a rapport with key reporters in order to sell them on the news value of your organization's activities.

Some argue that to serve well we must be, like lawyers, retained as outside counsel; *of* the organization rather than *in* it. In fact, we must be both. We must be able to explain to a reporter why we may *not* be able to give out certain information, and a few minutes later argue equally convincingly with an organization officer as to why we *should* disclose it. Representing at diffrent times the perspective of the reporter, the public and the organization, we become the official split personality. It is a much more difficult and more interesting role. Like Alice going through the looking glass, after this experience you will never view the world around you in the same way.

We hope *On Deadline* will help all of you present and future media relations practitioners to do a better job of walking the tightrope as you strive to balance a reporter's demand for fast and accurate information with the organization's need to guard competitive secrets and avoid violating the privacy of employees; as you work to become as adept at bringing valuable information into the organization as you are at getting the news out. For the beginner it will serve as a textbook; for the more experienced person, a reference book. But for neither should it be dull. Media relations is an exhilarating field. If our prose reflects the excitement of being part of news events as they unfold—and contributes to more accurate coverage of the activities of corporations and other organizations—then we will have adequately achieved our objectives and served our profession.

ACKNOWLEDGMENTS

Deciding who to thank when you work with colleagues and journalists who are so willing to share ideas and experiences is a very difficult task. However, there were some who were especially helpful with editorial advice, manuscript reviews, and unflagging interest from the time we got the initial idea to the day *On Deadline* was published: These include Chester Burger, Bob Burke, Hal Burlingame, Bill Cooper, Bob Ehinger, Roy Foltz, Dave Manahan, Brian Monahan, Bill Mullane, Elizabeth Park, Jack Sauchelli, Deb Stahl, Mike Tarpey, Al Wann and Candy Young. We also want to pay tribute to Mary Sokol, whose magic fingers kept us on our toes as well as on schedule. Above all, our gratitude to Bob, our parents and our families, whose belief in us has never wavered.

1

NEWS

What It Is and
How It Gets to the Public

A company newspaper once interviewed some construction workers at a site in Texas, asking each the questions: "How much of what you read in newspapers and what you see on television news shows do you believe? Why?"

An equipment foreman ended his answer with the statement: "We only get to see and hear what they [the news media] want us to."[1]

That answer could, in essence, be a definition of *news*.

If information does not get past the final editor's desk, it does not get printed, it does not get read on radio or shown on television and thus, it does not become reported news.

Such editorial processing of information is not unique to the news media. All of us make decisions each day, about which pieces of information we will keep to ourselves and which pieces we will share with peers, subordinates, superiors, families and friends. It is a natural process that appears innocent except when in the hands of news media personnel; in that arena, the process is determined to be one of power wielding.

For the professional media relations representative, the chore is not the delivery of news to an editor but, instead, the delivery of properly prepared material that might be passed on by an editor to become news.

But what criteria do editors use in determining whether or not material will become news?

Michigan State University conducted a survey for the American Society of Newspaper Editors and the Newspaper Readership Project to answer that question. The journalists queried defined news as having the following characteristics:

1. *Consequence*. Educates and informs; is important to lifestyle or ability to cope; has a moral or social importance; is "should know" material
2. *Interest*. Material is unusual, entertaining, has human interest, arouses emotions, or would cause people to talk about it
3. *Timeliness*. Material is current; is a new angle on events, or a new trend
4. *Proximity*. Pertains to local issues, trends, or events
5. *Prominence*. Concerns famous people, famous events; has received other media coverage[2]

From another perspective, that of a public relations textbook, news is "anything timely that is interesting and significant to readers or viewers."

One handbook on media relations gives two definitions of news: (*a*) the first information about any event that interests a large number of people; and (*b*) not what you want to tell other people but what other people want to know about you.

Still another definition is the one credited to an editor of the defunct *New York Sun*: "When a dog bites a man, that's not news. But if a man bites a dog, *that* is news."

The *Public Relations Journal* reports a change in the concept of news: "For the TV networks, news encompasses more than just major headlines. It also includes human-interest stories, entertainment, sports, fashion, and even food news. This broad-spectrum approach is found on the evening TV news and in newspapers as well. It is no longer unusual, for example, to see Dan Rather or Tom Brokaw reporting on a human-interest story such as the demise of a small mining town, the lastest fashion shows in Paris, or the return to popularity of American softball."[3]

Whichever definition you choose, remember this: news is a perishable commodity. Nothing is deader than yesterday's news.

For the media relations practitioner who has been given the edict to "Get this news out to the papers right away," determining if that material has a chance of becoming news can be easy.

Basically, there are five questions you can ask yourself about the material. These questions correlate well with what most journalists believe to be news criteria:

1. Is the story local? Does it have a local "hook" to it, something that will interest readers or viewers in this area?
2. Is this information unique or unusual?
3. Is the material timely? Is this something happening now or that will happen in the near future? Does the material relate to another item that is currently being discussed publicly?
4. Does this information concern people? (Our curiosity about the lives and events of others is evidenced by the strong sales of periodicals devoted just to people.)
5. Does this material create human interest? Pathos? Humor?

If the answer to any of these questions is yes, chances are your material will get an editor's attention and perhaps be placed in the newspaper or on the evening news.

HARD VERSUS SOFT NEWS

News generally falls into one of two categories: hard or soft.

Hard news most often happens by itself. An explosion or fire is hard news. The results of a board meeting can be hard news. A strike at the plant is hard news. This is news that the public needs to know. Soft news, on the other hand, is news that the public does not have to know. Soft news is a story about a couple who have been foster parents to 50 children. It is the dedication of a fountain in the park. It is the story of a blind operator at a switchboard. Soft news also is called "evergreen" because it is considered timeless and does not have to be used today, whereas hard news must be used immediately or it perishes.

Media relations practitioners probably will find, if they examine their placement activities, that they deal most often with soft news. Hard news items which must be planned for and placed each year can be determined easily: annual meeting results, quarterly earnings, election of new officers, opening a new office, or announcing a new product. Such items constitute a small percentage of the practitioner's time. The bulk of work likely deals with soft news placement, trying to interest the media in timeless material which can inform, educate or entertain readers or viewers.

Many practitioners fall down in the soft news placement part of their job because of the preconceived notion that the media would not be interested in the story of a company-sponsored fishing tournament or the planning involved in setting up a major exhibition of agency services. To keep from falling into this trap, remember that what may be "old hat" to you because of familiarity, may be considered news by an editor unfamiliar with your organization. If a story idea passes the five-question test outlined previously, it could become news.

PRINT VERSUS ELECTRONIC

A word of caution is needed. One story idea may not appeal to all media. That applies to hard news as well as soft news.

Quarterly sales results, for example, are considered hard news, but figures and percentages should be *seen* to be best understood. Newspapers and magazines may have the space to run this material but a television assignment editor probably will decide the information is not worth the effort to create the graphics nor the time needed to explain the material. Radio editors may also decide the material will take too much time in an already crowded newscast.

Conversely, a story idea about a picnic for disabled children may get excellent response from television because of its visual appeal, get no response from radio because of lack of imagery capabilities, and mild response from print media because of the amount of space needed to create empathy with the project through feature writing or still photography.

The key, of course, is to carefully determine which medium should be connected with which piece of material.

LOOKING FOR NEWS

Whether you are a full-time, part-time or volunteer media relations representative, the way to find news in your organization is to become a reporter. If you think with the mind of a reporter, someone trained to ask questions, you will find that you are constantly coming across story ideas.

Do not just accept the existence of your company's cafeteria, for example. Examine it. Why is it there? How are meals planned? How do the cafeteria personnel know how many people to anticipate each day? What kind of training is needed to work there? How has the service changed in the past 10 years to meet the increasing demand for more nutritional diets? Who creates the decorative pieces?

Do not assume that personnel news would not be used. Promotions into high office are newsworthy not just to the business, financial, or trade press, but also to the person's hometown papers, alumni magazines, and professional society journals. Notices of service anniversaries, training courses completed, retirements, and honors received are welcome at various publications; the trick is to match the medium with the message. Some of these items, depending on visual appeal, could interest television as well.

An excellent source of story material about your organization is the internal newsletter or newspaper. Sending this publication out to editors in your area often will generate a flow of activity as the media seek to expand a story or get a different angle on it.

Items covered in an internal publication that could interest journalists include:

1. *Suggestion award winners.* Rewarding an employee for ingenious thinking makes for a good story beyond the company gates.

2. *Company-sponsored blood drives.* Finding out who has donated the most blood, for the most number of years can help an editor get a story idea. Perhaps you have employees with rare blood types. Perhaps there is an employee who has traced his/her donation to see who received it.

3. *Unusual hobbies.* The significant word here is "unusual" because a hobby truly must be that before an editor will consider

the idea. However, almost every employee has a hobby and the possibility exists that some are some unusual.

4. *Unusual jobs.* Not all jobs are glamorous, nor are they dull and boring. There are, within most organizations, jobs that do not fit the normal mold. Within AT&T Technologies, there is one person at a manufacturing facility in Louisiana who tests coin telephones by constantly inserting coins. The job has been written about numerous times and has been shown on local and network television programs.

5. *Service projects sponsored by the company or by the employee clubs.* Employee clubs often will have a designated person to contact media about these projects but the company media relations person could be nearby as well to serve as a consultant.

6. *Introduction of new equipment.* The age of technology brings with it an abundance of items about new, labor-saving devices. Depending on the device and its function, there might be a story.

7. *Seasonal events.* Special activities planned for Thanksgiving or Christmas should be brought to the media's attention as soon as possible. There are more organizations wanting to highlight their activities than there are media slots in which to place them. Look for what makes your activity different or unique.

8. *Production records.* Turning out the zillionth widget can be an item worth noting if your organization is the first to make a zillion widgets, or if you did so in record time. For the nonprofit area, there can be production records in terms of time, numbers of people served, or other units of measurement.

9. *Construction news.* If your organization is building anew or renovating, information about the progress may be welcomed by the media as a possible visual story or, at the very least, a reminder that a story will be coming when the work is completed.

10. *Visiting dignitaries.* If a home office executive is visiting the local plant and can make appearances or be available for interviews, the media would like to know. The same holds true for national or international officers of civic or professional organizations.

11. *Organization milestones.* There are always anniversaries of one kind or another to commemorate; often, these dates will be

relevant to the community or offer an opportunity to reflect on changes brought about by your company or service organization.

This list is far from complete, but it does show the possibilities for news that already exist within your organization.

Coming up with a list of story ideas that can be presented to editors is like preparing a menu: there will always be certain offerings for customers and there should also be house specials to entice that customer to return. Do not be discouraged, however, if the editor decides he or she does not want anything from your offering today; tomorrow, that same editor may decide your fare is the best in town.

DIRECTING YOUR STORY TO THE RIGHT MEDIUM

"A newspaper is as much a product as an automobile or a pair of shoes. A product must be good if it is to sell, but the selling features of each particular product make the difference between it and its competition."[4]

Too many media relations professionals forget that television shows, periodicals and radio newscasts are products and not services. As a result of this initial misunderstanding, these professionals often try to market the wrong story to the wrong product—or medium.

One way to help direct your stories to the best possible medium is to break that medium down into its component parts—or products. Understanding the selling features of a medium's product will help you more carefully place your story. Editors will appreciate your understanding of their marketing process and will doubly appreciate that you are not wasting their time.

Starting with five main media categories, you can develop your own selection list for the particular media that you wish to attract.

Newspapers

Whether published weekly or daily, newspapers are divided by sections: national/international news, sports, business, entertainment, home living, science, real estate and other sections.

Knowing who makes the decisions for each section, what the requirements are for that section and the schedule for the section's production are prerequisites to deciding where you should attempt to place items. It is possible that one story might have several angles and could be of interest to several section editors. For example, the business editor would want to know the financial impact of your company's new product announcement and how it relates to the local business community. If it is a consumer product, the home or leisure editor would be interested in knowing what the product does for the customer.

Each editor serves a different constituency and is interested only in what each item means in terms of the interests of that constituency.

Newspapers also have columnists, local and/or syndicated, who specialize in areas that may support the sections or reflect the general editorial stance of the newspaper. Columnists can be strong selling features for newspapers, so getting to know them is important.

A columnist writing on economics is a good target for an in-depth explanation relating to new pricing policies for your industry's products or services. The columnist in the family section who provides household hints wants only "how-to" material and cannot use detailed or lengthy background information. The columnist catering to farmers and gardeners would be interested in your company's new herbicide.

When marketing to a newspaper a story that has several angles or possibilities, make sure each editor, columnist, or writer knows you are talking to the others. You should never assume that internal communications on a newspaper are at peak efficiency and if your story appears twice in the same edition, you have lost your credibility.

Newsletters

Newsletters have become a popular medium in a world crowded with publications. Their rise can be partially attributed to the format of the medium. Newsletters offer bite-sized chunks of information in a small publication that can be easily stored or—just as easily—tossed away.

Because of their brevity, newsletters can concentrate on one specific topic within a broad area of interest, or can be devoted to a particular broad issue. For example, you might find a newsletter written for investors in petroleum products only, and another designed for all investors.

Newsletter staffs are small and generally appreciate your news releases and story offerings as long as the information is geared to the newsletter audience. In serving newsletters, you should inquire about the possible use of photographs or graphics.

Magazines

The proliferation of specialized magazines is making placement in this medium easier in terms of identification but more difficult in terms of quantity.

The first step is to identify which magazines reach your particular audiences. You may have to compile several breakout lists if your media operation is extensive. For instance, you may find you need magazines that reach your customers (by level of decision-making, by geography, by financial status), your industry (by specific area of technology, services, support), or the public at large (for business, leisure, product or consumer issues).

Like the newspapers, each magazine may then be divided into sections. However, because the magazine itself serves a special constituency, there will not be as much subdivision.

The same rules of careful analysis apply to magazines with one added feature: magazines are candidates to run photographs supplied by you. Often, a photograph of a new product or one representing a new service may be run as a stand-alone piece if there is not room for the entire story. Check the magazine's requirements carefully, however, to avoid sending a product photograph to a publication that never uses them.

Many of the trade magazines run special issues or annuals in conjunction with trade shows or fairs. These may be the targets for which you aim specifically instead of trying to broadside a publication throughout the year.

Radio

Radio is perhaps the least complex of the media; and, very possibly, is the most overlooked.

Radio stations are following the trend of print by specializing and appealing to distinct, segmented audiences. This audio specialization produces a good product for the radio station but can frustrate the media relations professional who does not take the time to thoroughly investigate the medium.

The broadcast range of radio stations is an important factor for you to know. The stations with the widest, most powerful ranges are the ones you need if you have an emergency, such as an urgent call for blood at your hospital, or updating the public on a chemical spill that may necessitate evacuation.

You need these power stations no matter what kind of music they play! Your personal preference may not lean towards country music, hard rock or classical, but if you need powerful broadcasting strength, go to the source.

You need to determine the product line of each station to help you decide which stations to cater to at which times. There are all-news stations, all-classical stations, all-country stations and all easy-listening stations. The majority of stations are a mix of talk, music, commentary, news, sports, special programming—each station trying to find its niche in a rapidly growing radio audience.

Most radio stations manage with small news operations. They depend primarily on material that comes over the wire services, is delivered to the station, or is called in to the news director. All radio stations, large and small, like to use "actualities" to liven up the newscast.

An actuality is a live or taped comment from you or some other organization spokesperson. Being willing and available to provide an actuality will often enhance your position vis-à-vis the radio news director who makes the decision about your story offering.

Stations that offer call-in talk shows may be of interest to you if your organization is involved in a sensitive or volatile issue and you need to set the record straight or respond to the public's concerns.

Specialized radio programs also offer opportunities to present subject-matter experts talking about consumer items, technology and farm-related topics.

Talk with radio news directors and program directors to get detailed information on a station's opportunities. Then target your material carefully to a listening audience. For example, early morning and late afternoon talk shows can have a large "driving" audience of automobile commuters.

Television

Because television offers both sound and sight, and because the industry is fragmenting its audiences through cable television channels, a media relations specialist must approach this medium with a totally new perspective.

Whereas most people believe they get their news from television, television news shows account for only a small percentage of the station's offerings. Supporting the newscasts are network shows, locally produced variety/entertainment/talk shows, syndicated specials, live, network-produced coverage of events, documentaries, and movies.

Unless you are in charge of national media for your organization, you should be concerned primarily with locally produced shows for your story and news offerings.

The local news shows are the prime targets for your releases. Assignment editors at the television station determine which stories will be covered for the evening news. They make the determination based partially on the real news value of the item and partially on its visual qualities. Television is a *motion* picture medium, which means that your news or story idea should have with it ways in which the story can be shown. A slide of the president of your company may be visual, ,but it gets dull after just a few seconds because it does not move. If your item is short, then the slide may be all that is needed. Decide carefully if you can visually support your soft news story before offering it to television news.

Local talk shows provide an excellent medium for your subject-matter experts, if they are well trained, to talk about, demonstrate and respond to issues. The show's producer can give you more detailed information about the requirements for the show, time needed for booking of guests and capability for live demonstrations.

The new cable offerings provide a magazine menu in video form. It will continue to be much easier now to reach segmented audiences down to the community level with video feature-story ideas, in-depth coverage of issues and public service offerings.

Cable television provides channels on health, sports, news, music, religion, country music, movies, and many other interests. Geography can determine whether there will be an additional channel in a foreign language; for example, Spanish in the western states which border Mexico. Working closely with your in-house video production team, you can provide to certain cable channels programs produced by your organization to meet your target audiences.

DIRECTORIES AND MAILING LISTS

With the profusion of new media concepts comes the potential difficulty of tracking each medium, editor, writer, schedule and requirement.

There are numerous directories available to a media relations practitioner. They can cover print and electronic media, from international to local levels. Determining which directory best suits your needs may take some time and study but will be well worth the effort.

A first step might be to visit the public library to peruse the directories available there. In looking through the media directories, ask yourself these questions and any others you can think of that suit your specific situation:

1. How often is the directory printed? Updated?
2. What geographic region(s) does it cover?
3. Does it include trade publications? Specialty magazines?
4. Does it list radio and television?
5. Does it give the names of editors? Columnists?
6. Are there editorial and photo guidelines?
7. What is the circulation for the publication listed?
8. What is the viewing audience for television and the listening audience for radio?
9. Does the directory list television talk shows?

As a check on what you select from the directory, talk with the marketing people in your organization if you have such a department. They can show you which trade publications they think are important. From that, you can get names of editors and write for editorial and photo criteria if they are, not listed in the publication.

Also, you should talk with your advertising department or agency. Clearly you need to at least coordinate and preferably integrate your editorial media strategies with those of the advertising group. After all, your organization does not normally advertise in publications that do not reach a critical buying audience. While you cannot use advertising as a political tool on which to base editorial placements, you can at least know that you are attempting to reach a key audience.

Ultimately, you will want to create your own directory. In doing so, try to create the listing in a way that best reflects your media efforts. For example, if you deal almost exclusively with business news, you probably will not need a listing of sports editors. Your breakouts can be in various categories and even cross-referenced by geography, business publication or broadcast capabilities.

One directory breakout could look like this:

   I. Local
      A. Business publications
         1. Magazines
         2. Newspapers
         3. Newsletters
      B. TV Business Broadcasts
      C. Radio Business Broadcasts
      D. Wire Services
  II. National
      A. Business Publications
         1. Magazines
         2. Newspapers
         3. Newsletters
      B. TV Business Broadcasts
      C. Radio Business Broadcasts
      D. Wire Services
 III. International
      A. Business Publications
         1. Magazines
         2. Newsletters
      B. Wire Services

Under each category should go *all* the information you can possible get about each publication, electronic show or service. Perhaps the most important item is the name of the person with whom you will most often communicate. Remember, you do not deal with newspapers or television, you deal with people.

Some of the information you will need is:

1. Name of publication/station/show/service
2. Name of editor/reporter/columnist
3. Street address (for delivering packages)
4. Mailing address (for ordinary correspondence)
5. Telephone number(s)
6. Telex number(s)
7. Facsimile number(s)
8. Deadline(s)
9. Photography requirements
10. Use of actuality
11. Circulation
12. Broadcast range
13. Times of pertinent broadcasts

Directories should be updated constantly. Keeping a directory on a word processor is one way to make this chore easier but there is nothing wrong with writing in the changes and updates by hand as you get them. The important thing is to have available an easy-to-use and fully functional directory.

Clearly, determining what news is and where it should be directed involves more than just writing a release and sending it to every medium in your area. Careful analysis of the information itself and the media to which it should be directed will help you achieve your media goals.

CHAPTER

2 GETTING STARTED

Setting Up Your Program

Getting started in media relations means understanding your role and your objectives and sticking to both.

But what is your role? Referee? Propagandizer? Shuffler of news releases?

One fact that few executives or organization leaders seem to appreciate is that your role is to make a reporter's job easy, help that reporter meet his or her objectives and, at the same time, help your organization meet its objectives.

This tightrope-walking exercise means that when you speak to a reporter you are representing the organization; when you speak to the people in your organization you are representing the reporter.

You do not need a split personality to achieve the balance. But, you do need a sound understanding of everyone's goals and objectives. The reporter's objective is to get a story to help his or her management meet a goal of having a newspaper that will sell or a television newscast that will attract viewers. Now, what are your goals and objectives?

WHAT KIND OF PROGRAM?

There are two possible kinds of media relations programs: passive and active.

15

A passive program means that your organization has determined, for whatever reason, to not seek the attention of the public eye. Privately held companies sometimes engage in this practice and can do so because they are not forced by law or regulation to divulge earnings or other financial data.

A passive posture may be initially frustrating to reporters but, once the word gets around, the organization generally is left alone, except in crises. Any other mention in the media about such a company often is speculation.

Even an organization obligated to divulge information to the public can still have a passive program. In this case, nothing beyond what must be reported is given out. This stance does not win friends among the media but if the respect of journalists is not a goal, the stance is okay. There is no need for a media relations person in such an organization because attorneys and accountants can prepare the basic required releases for the public.

If, however, you are with an organization that wishes to have an active media relations program, you need to understand what *active* means. Perhaps, more importantly, you need to know that *active does not mean*:

> Churning out a release a day
> Taking reporters to lunch all the time
> Holding a news conference at the drop of a hat
> Scheduling all of your subject-matter experts on every radio and television talk show in your area
> Counting inches of copy or seconds of air time as the sole measurement technique

Active does mean that you plan, implement and measure a well-conceived media relations program that supports your organization's goals and objectives. The way to do this is to set up your own media relations goals, objectives, strategies and timetables.

WRITING IT DOWN

The first step in this process is to know well the direction in which your organization is headed. This means knowing its mission, goals, and objectives. You then can create your own program.

First, look at each of the organization's goals carefully. Then, write down all the ways in which you can help your organization meet those goals.

For example, if your organization is like most, it will have a goal concerning finances. It may be a declared statement about the amount of return on investment or it may be a desire not to have to raise members' dues. Your support could include a series of briefings for financial analysts, placement of articles relating to organizational growth in magazines that reach investor audiences, or making sure the public knows of the many services your organization provides.

Another organizational goal probably relates to human resources: the intention to maintain a well-trained, well-paid, employee universe with a low percentage of turnover. If you think this is an internal matter only, you should ask yourself where the employees come from. They come from the public at large.

Your role in this area can be to make sure the public is aware of what a good place your organization is to work for by issuing announcements of promotions, retirements, long-term service anniversaries, suggestion award winners, employee club activities, plant/office improvements, and corporate donations.

This exercise of writing down ideas helps you marshall your thoughts, ensure you truly do understand your organization's key objectives, and understand how you can fit into an overall structure. Take that list of ideas and put them aside since they will be used later.

THE FORMAL STRUCTURE

There are any number of ways in which to structure your media relations program. Select the way that best suits the day-to-day management techniques, language, and operations of your organization. The following example may be of help, however:

Media Relations Program: XYZ COMPANY

Goal I.   To support the company's goal to attain financial stability through increased investments by the public.

    1. *Objective:* To provide the financial media with timely, accurate earnings information.

Strategies
a. Establish contact with key person in Finance Department who will provide information to media relations department on pre-arranged schedule.
b. Create a checklist of financial reporters in general, also business and trade publications that reach targeted audience.
c. Prepare questions and answers in advance that journalists might ask about organization's finances.

2. *Objective:* To help encourage targeted audiences to invest in the organization by making them aware of the solvency and growth of the company.
   Strategies
   a. Determine the key investor audiences by working with the investor relations department.
   b. Determine which publications or types of publications those audiences are likely to read.
   c. Attempt to place six articles in those publications which reflect the growth of the company.

3. *Objective:* To help financial media have better understanding of the organization's future.
   Strategies
   a. Select three key financial writers who reach an influential target audience.
   b. Arrange for each writer to have an interview with a selected specialist in the Finance Department; each interview to occur at separate times, covering separate stories.
   c. Mail updated information kits to all financial journalists on the mailing list.

Goal II. To support the organization's goal of hiring and maintaining a well-trained employee body with a low percentage of turnover.

1. *Objective:* To inform the public of the accomplishments of long-term employees.
   Strategies
   a. Work with personnel, establish a way to be notified of all personnel advancements and retirements.
   b. Create a brief form to be filled out by each promoted or retiring employee that will give information to be used in a news release.
   c. Upon notification of promotion, issue release to

        selected business media within five days. Issue release to employee's hometown papers and his/her alumni magazine within two weeks.

    d. Upon notification of retiring employee, issue release to business and trade press, hometown papers and alumni publications at least two weeks before retirement date.

  2. *Objective:* To show the organization as a good corporate citizen.

    Strategies

    a. Compile a list of all employees involved in civic and volunteer activities.

    b. Select possible feature-story ideas from that list.

    c. Interview the employee and his/her supervisor about the activities.

    d. Try to place the resulting story in area weekly newspapers, or sell the story idea (if visual) to the local television station.

While the XYZ Company example is somewhat simplistic and altruistic, it does show that a media relations program can be planned with concise and written goals, objectives, and strategies. Of course, each strategy should have a specific timeframe included with it.

When the plan is completed, it should be sent to the key executives in your organization for review and comment. This action accomplishes a number of items.

First, it shows your top management that you are attuned to the workings of your organization because your departmental activities are geared to support the entire organization and its objectives.

Second, it allows each person the opportunity to have some input to the plan. Everyone likes to be asked his or her opinion of something; most people like to respond with a suggested change or two. A word of caution: Do not automatically incorporate all suggestions into your plan. Look at each suggestion and, as objectively as possible, consider both its source and what happens to related activities if it is incorporated.

The reason to take some time with these suggestions is that not everyone sees the world in the same way. Thus, the vice president of labor relations will have concerns quite different from the vice president of financial relations who, in turn, will have ideas different from the vice president of marketing who will differ widely with the general attorney.

Understanding each person's viewpoint will help you understand the suggestion he or she made. At that point, you can see what the implications might be if you automatically incorporate that person's suggestion about your media program. You may find that all suggestions are actual improvements on your plan; you may find that none of the suggestions will improve the plan but that they reflect the concerns of the person making the suggestion.

After incorporating any new data, make sure these same people see the final document labeled as your "working document." This is the plan from which you will work day by day. This also is the basis for the measurement of your program and your individual performance. Each person on the media relations staff should have a copy of the final plan as well. It should be referred to often and updated regularly.

If you and your staff think of the media plan as a "List of Things To Do," it will help bring that plan into the day-to-day reality of the job. We all know the satisfaction we get from crossing through an item on that infamous list; the same holds true with a well-written plan because you can cross off each strategy and, ultimately, each objective on the list.

GETTING THE OFFICE PREPARED

Generally speaking, not enough effort is spent in outfitting a media relations office. Much time and frustration could be saved if more preparation were put into the physical items needed in your working area. If you were a dentist you would not open up shop without the proper equipment, would you? And a lawyer would not think of hanging out a shingle without making sure the necessary reference books were nearby.

The physical equipment for media relations may be determined by the way in which your business operates. You may get a trusty manual typewriter or the latest in word processors, if that is how your company thinks. You will need plenty of filing space and work space; a large desk capable of handling several pieces of paper at a time is nice.

The telephone system is important. Reporters should never be frustrated in their attempts to reach you because your line is busy. You need either more than one line to your office or successive lines that automatically jump over to a secretary's or subordinate's line for pickup when your line is busy. Whatever system you select, remember that the objective is to make sure a reporter can reach you when he/she wants to—not when it is convenient for you.

Your office should be a veritable library of resource information. Among the books and materials that should be sitting on your shelves are:

1. An up-to-date dictionary
2. A style manual
3. A thesaurus
4. Your organization's annual reports for the past five years
5. Professional journals/books relating to media relations
6. Company-produced material, such as recruitment brochures, product promotion material, benefits booklets
7. Copies of your organization's internal publications
8. Media directories
9. Organization charts
10. History of the organization (if one doesn't exist, consider writing it)
11. Company statistics
12. Calendar of events for the organization (earnings releases, product announcements, speeches to be given by the president)
13. Press kits (keep about 25 available at all times)
14. Business cards
15. Corporate goals and objectives/media goals and objectives
16. An atlas

All of this material is used, at some time, in some way. Reporters can ask obscure questions and you have to be ready to reply as quickly as possible.

Of key importance is the compilation of company/organization statistics. Journalists seem to adore numbers: they are easy to read, easy to compare, work well in headlines, and impress readers. So, get a head start on potential questions involving numbers by thinking of those questions yourself. The result should be a file on statistics that includes such items as:

1. *Employee numbers.* These should be broken down by management/non-mangement, union/non-union, male/female, growth over the years, percentage increases in different universes, location/geography, number of years of employment

2. *Physical plants.* How many plants do you have? How much square footage is that? If it is really large, how many total acres is that? When was each plant built? Who were the architects? What are the details of each opening (who cut the ribbon, who was guest speaker, first workers)? Who decides where to buy/build a plant?

3. *Miscellaneous information.* What are the key dates in your organization's history? What employee served the longest period of time? What is your best production record? What are the odd hobbies among your employee body?

4. *Executive information.* What are the biographical data on each of your organization's executives? If it is a large group, from where did most of them graduate? Were they all in the service? How many have advanced degrees?

Because you do not know until the phone rings what might be on a reporter's mind, it is best to start gathering all this material together now. And keep adding to it all the time. One of the most convenient ways we have found to store this material is with binders (unless you are lucky enough to have a terminal on your desk with access to all the computerized information dealing with your organization).

Binders make it easy to store and retrieve material without the papers getting damaged in a regular file. If labeled properly, they can be easily seen in a bookshelf, even from across a room; they can be indexed for easy reference.

Whichever method you may select, remember the object is to have material at hand that you can get to quickly and easily when a reporter asks you a question. A reporter will remember you if you are able to respond immediately without having to say "I'll get back to you on that."

This is also a good time to begin compiling your list of subject-matter experts within your organization.

This list actually is your organization list in reverse.

When reporters call for an interview or just to get some general information, they do not begin by asking to speak specifically to "Mr. Jones, the manager of personnel statistics." Instead, the reporter is more likely to ask you if he/she can speak with "someone who can talk about personnel statistics." The reporter does not know the people in your company—that is your job.

So, start a list of subject-matter experts by thinking like a reporter and asking yourself: who is knowledgable about pricing policies? Labor relations? Purchasing? Individual products? Transportation services? Food services? Financial statistics?

If you list the subjects alphabetically, and then beside each entry list the subject-matter expert (with telephone numbers), you may find your job much easier the next time a reporter calls.

INTRODUCING YOURSELF

Now that you have a media relations plan and a well-coordinated office, it is time to start letting the media know who you are.

With your media relations plan in mind, you need to select the persons within the media that you need to meet. Do not assume that you have to know all the editors and program directors at all the newspapers, magazines, and television and radio stations in a 500-mile radius.

You should select only those media, and only those editors, who can help you meet your goals and objectives. Those are the people critical to your efforts. Once you have made that list, you do not rush out and attempt to call on all persons at once, nor do you automatically call and invite each one to lunch. Instead, take the time to think about what you want to do and plan your activity accordingly. If none of the editors know you because you are new to the job and/or new to the area, then your primary reason for contact is just to get to know these people.

Select your list of people and begin calling to set up appointment times when you can go by and introduce yourself. Make sure you call at the least busy times: after the newspaper has been put to bed, after the television crews have received their assignments and have gone on location, after the radio newscast. In making these appointments, you should ask for just a brief amount of time. Do not try to crowd all your appointments into the same day because you also want to be on time for each appointment.

As you meet each editor or program director, present them with some basic material on you and your organization. An information kit filled with the most recent annual report, a fact sheet, and a copy of your president's very best or most recent speech makes a nice introductory package. Include in that package several of your business cards (make sure your home telephone number appears) and perhaps even some slides or photographs of your chief executives and one of your company logo.

You should not try to sell something on this first trip out. Your objectives at this time are to let the media know you, to recognize you and to know how to reach you. If you come asking for air time or editorial consideration, you could be considered a hard-line salesperson instead of a media relations professional.

The personal contact should be maintained throughout the year in various ways. Do not wait until you need the media to be on your side in a tough situation.

If you can not personally visit each editor, reporter, or program director occasionally, at least keep up with them by telephone or by dropping a note to them. One way to do this is to have these people put on the mailing list for your employee publication. This keeps the company in the editor's mind and also provides an opportunity for that editor to come up with his or her own ideas for stories.

Another way to enjoy contact without compromise is to join, if it is possible, a local press club or some other association frequented by the news media.

Also, you may want to attend workshops, seminars, or lectures conducted by the news media. This gives you the benefit of learning more about this audience that you serve while, at the same time, you let the media know by your presence that you take your position seriously and professionally.

MEANWHILE, BACK AT THE OFFICE ...

If you are out meeting the media, attending lectures, and dropping by the press club, who is minding the store?

Office coverage, both when you are there and when you are

not, is another element of media relations that is too often overlooked. Such an omission courts disaster.

You must, in essence, be prepared to serve the media 24 hours a day, 7 days a week. The people who work for you must understand that and they must be knowledgeable in how to help you serve the media. Reporters working for the morning newspaper must be able to reach you during evening hours. A television newscaster might need you before the eleven o'clock news. Radio could need you any hour on the hour. If you deal with international media, compound this by numerous time zones.

As we have stated before, and shall again because it is so important, make sure your home telephone number is on all your business cards and news releases. If that home number changes, that is a good reason to contact all your media to notify them of the change.

Consider including a telex number on cards and releases as well. This works well with media from around the world or across several time zones; questions can be asked and answered via telex instead of the telephone.

Make sure your office staff knows how to handle any media inquiry. They will need to get the name of the reporter (accurately!), the name of the media he or she represents, the telephone number where the reporter can be reached (check that number twice), the deadline under which the reporter is working, and the nature of the request. In short, you are attempting to get any of the same information that would normally be requested of a caller. With a reporter, however, the timing is often more critical.

When you issue a release, make sure that you, or the person listed on the release as the contact person, is at the office through late afternoon to catch any calls from reporters working the morning papers or from television news directors for the evening news. The effort you just expended on issuing that release is wasted if you leave the office at 4:30 P.M. and the journalists do not come on their beat or shift until later. They may try to reach you at home but, if you are a commuter, you have some dead time between leaving the office and reaching your home.

Also make sure that during lunch there is always someone to answer the media department's telephones. You know from personal experience the frustration of hearing a telephone ring for some minutes, especially a telephone you know should be answered because it is a business number. You also know that your opinion of the people at the other end of the line decreases in direct proportion to the number of times the telephone rings. You work very hard building credibility with the media; do not let it disappear because everyone went to lunch at the same time.

There is an adage that says "Failing to plan is planning to fail." This is true of most things, but we think it especially proves itself with media relations.

Whether you are setting up a year's program, a visit with an editor, office coverage, or a delivery system of news releases, planning will help you do your job more efficiently, more quickly, and with more assurance. Thus, with planning you should attain your objectives, one of which is to help the reporter meet his/her objectives.

TOOLS OF THE TRADE

From News Releases to Background Briefings

When you are young and just starting out on your own, someone—perhaps a kindly uncle—gives you a small box of tools, with the gentle admonition: "You never know when these might come in handy."

Most of us take a scoffing look at the tool kit, figuring we can get through life with, at most, a flathead screwdriver or, on rare occasion, a Phillips head screwdriver. We continue to feel that way until the day arrives when we find we really do need that funny thing with the whatchamacallit on the end. At that point, we offer silent thanks to our kindly uncle.

The tool kit for the beginning media relations person offers many items, some familiar and of day-to-day use, others obscure and needed only for the trickiest of chores.

NEWS RELEASES

Of the many ways to get into the media, the most commonly known and the most often misused is the news release. The cries of editors seem to be heard only in the wilderness as practitioners repeat mistakes under the guise of "But, my release is different."

If, indeed, that release is different, the information contained therein will appear in the newspaper, magazine, or on radio or television.

Most releases are not different, according to those in the know; in other words, the editors. The over-surveyed guardians of the media repeatedly cite horror stories of illiteracy, cutesy-poo press kits, out-of-date mailing lists, material missing the local angle, missing information, an abundance of meaningless management commentary, and still more illiteracy.

News releases are not designed to take the place of a reporter. Instead, a news release is a for-your-information memorandum to an editor. A release simply acquaints an editor with the basic facts of a potential story, just as a memo would. The editor will then decide if the proposed story warrants attention, if so, a reporter is assigned to gather more information and rewrite the material to fit the format of the publication, radio, or television.

The idea, simply, is to get editors to read the release—a difficult task when editors are bombarded with pieces of paper only thinly disguised as news.

Just as a memorandum should be short and to the point, so too should a news release. There also are basic components to a release:

1. *The name of the organization.* There is no need to go overboard with multicolored flashing letters and brilliant ink. A simple company or association letterhead will suffice. The name tells the reader the source of the release and gives credibility to the information.

2. *Contact name and number.* At the top of the release should be the name of the person to call for more information. Underneath that should be both office and home telephone numbers (do not forget the area code or an "800" listing). For releases going to international media, a telex number is a must. The rationale for including several lines of contacts is simple: the media do not operate in a uniform nine-to-five day; even if they did, they are not all in the same time zone or the same country. Remember, also, that the pages of a news releases can become separated so it is a good idea to have the contact name on the last sheet of a release as well.

3. *A headline or tag line.* This piece of information is not

intended as a substitute for the publication's headline writer's efforts. Instead, it gives the reader a capsule phrase summing up the essence of the release. If this were the memorandum, the headline would be the same as the "Re." Consequently, the headline tells the reader if this is something that needs to be tended to right away or if it can wait.

4. *A release time.* This information, also at the top of the release, says when the information can be published or broadcast. It can read "Release upon receipt" or "Release immediately" or "Release Friday, December 16, 1984." If the release is embargoed, that is, it must not be released until a certain time, then that time must be specific, such as "For release after 2 P.M., Friday, December 16, 1984." A word of caution, however. Do not embargo information unless it is required. Editors know that embargoes on stories about a company picnic are juvenile attempts at making the information seem more important than it is. There are times when embargoes must be honored, editors know and respect those times.

5. *An ending.* Of course a release ends, but editors, copyreaders, and reporters are accustomed to looking for a "-30-" or "###" mark to say that the release is ended. Otherwise, a release that comes close to the bottom of a page could be misconstrued as only part of a longer story.

Those are the components of a release—the building blocks, as it were. Of equal importance is what the release says and how it says it.

Other suggestions for news releases are:

1. *Go easy on the length.* There are no hard and fast rules about the length of a release; however, two typewritten pages, double-spaced, is considered the approved length. If your release is several pages long, you may wish to consider either breaking it up into several releases, each dealing with a specific topic, or issuing a short release with a longer fact sheet accompanying it.

2. *Avoid breaks.* It makes for easier reading and more accurate typesetting if you do not split words at the end of a line or split a sentence at the bottom of a page.

3. *Clear writing.* Writing a release in corporate jargon, legalese or some other alien language, makes as much sense as

preparing a release in French and sending it to people who speak only English. Why? As an AT&T executive once cautioned writers: "I have used lawyer-talk out of what seemed to me to be necessary care for accuracy and safety. And it comes out the other end as a credibility gap."

4. *Remember the pyramid.* The inverted pyramid style of writing is not used just for news releases. The same style applies in writing personal letters, memos, briefs, white papers and so forth. The important information is given first, with less important information following and, finally, the least important information at the end. Using the pyramid calls for a bit of taste, however. Although the lead paragraph of a release carries the most important information, it is not necessary to cram the answers to "Who? What? Where? Why? When? How?" into that first paragraph.

5. *Adjectives are dangerous.* Avoid the temptation to use superlatives in describing your organization's latest product, service or new executive. For one thing, such superlative claims may not be legally defensible; for another, use of adjectival claims hints that the writer had nothing of substance to say about the subject and threw in *spectacular* for lack of anything else.

6. *Make it local.* One of the key criteria listed for what sells a release to an editor is the local angle or "hook" it has. For example, a national release announcing a new product can be localized by telling when the product will be available in your area, through what outlet, and at what suggested retail price.

NEWS RELEASES FOR RADIO AND TELEVISION

Isn't a release always a release? No. Not when one is for print and another is for electronic media.

Both television and radio have special characteristics that require you to handle your release differently than if the release were going to print media.

Primarily, the difference is that radio news is written for the ear; television news is written for the eye and the ear; whereas print news is written for the eye only.

The best test for electronic news writing is to prepare the release as though it were going to be read directly from your paper. Then, read the release aloud to someone and ask him or her to re-tell the message. You may find a disparity between what you said and what was heard.

Broadcast style is not difficult, however. A few easy-to-remember rules will help you through:

1. Because the material is written to time and not space, everything must be spelled out. There can be no abbreviations, no numerals and all names or unusual words should be spelled phonetically.

2. Sentences are short, with descriptive words before rather than after nouns. For example, "the thirty-nine year-old vice president" instead of "the vice president, 39."

3. The inverted pyramid rule is not used in broadcast journalism. In print, a reader can go back and reread a paragraph or a sentence; in listening to the radio, a listener cannot go back. Radio and television journalism is linear. In broadcast style, the release tells what the news is, then tells it again, and then tells it again. Here is an example: "The Smith and Jones Company will build a new manufacturing plant here in Anytown. The new facility will employ 2000 people to make the latest in electronic devices. Smith and Jones' newest operation will be ready in two years, cost 5 million dollars, and add several thousand dollars a year to the local tax base." Three times, the fact that there will be a new plant was repeated to the listener.

4. For television, remember that the paramount consideration is visual interest. Your story about new ways to invest money for greater return *sounds* great and reads better but looks terrible with its charts, graphs, and "talking head" expert. In contrast, a story about a white-water rafting trip for children who have never been out of a city reads like many other stories, sounds like a bunch of squealing children against a backdrop of rushing water but, *looks* exciting, enticing and dangerous.

INTERVIEW

The interview, whether individual or at a press conference, is a highly successful tool. However, its sophistication calls for serious study and preparation. Chapter 5, "Spokespersons: Training and

Briefing Them For Their Role," provides the material you need to conduct a successful interview.

OP-ED PIECES

One of the newer tools to the media relations kit is the op-ed piece. Named for its position in a newspaper—opposite the editorial page—the op-ed piece provides a place where your organization can offer an opinion on a subject, or perhaps philosophize about a current issue.

Criteria for op-ed pieces will very widely as the form is still in embryonic stages in many places. The best advice is to read your local newspapers to determine their formats, and then call to ask for their specific rules.

There are some general criteria for op-ed pieces. On the average, op-ed pieces are run every day, from one article to two or three. The length appears most often to be about 750 words. Specifics may vary, but almost all op-ed editors agree whole-heartedly that the pieces must have two things: timeliness and creativity.

No editor likes to receive a piece that already has been run in some other publication, nor does that editor care to receive an article on an issue that has been dead for months. Some editors prefer to avoid controversial issues, feeling that adversary journalism can become like a ping-pong game. Others encourage publication of diverse opinions on sensitive subjects.

Topics for op-ed pieces are multitudinous, ranging from opinions and analyses of public affairs, politics, education and law, to journalism, health care, religion, and lifestyles. Topics can be of a local or national nature. But, they must be timely.

Some editors prefer to discuss the idea for an op-ed piece ahead of time, others prefer to receive the completed article with just a cover letter. There also may be constraints concerning copyright or usage.

Used judiciously, op-ed pieces can be the answer to many an executive's prayer. How often have you heard one of your management bemoan the fact that "The people just don't understand this issue!" The op-ed piece may help explain that issue to them.

Op-ed pieces are not to be used as a vendetta medium against some alleged injustice to your organization, nor are they the fora for challenging a reporter's techniques. The key word in considering op-ed pieces is *judicius*. Just define the issue you wish to discuss or state the problem as you see it, provide whatever background or history is needed, and then suggest ways the situation can be changed or improved.

TALK SHOWS

Whether on radio or television, talk shows present excellent opportunities for your media relations efforts. The programmers for these shows have to fill that time slot every day or every week; they are looking for ideas, for guests, for the unusual. You, on the other hand, have an abundance of ideas and people available to provide to the programmer. Also, radio and television must present public service programs to keep their licenses; it is a wise media relations person who takes advantage of this arrangement.

Radio talk shows give you and your organization the opportunity to present a new program, or a twist to an old program, or even to present your views on a ticklish issue.

The possible thorn in this is that the call-in variety talk show gets more listeners but also presents some dangers. Even the best-trained spokesperson in your organization is likely to get riled at questions such as "Do you still beat your wife?" which can come on talk shows. Before agreeing to participate in such a program, listen to several of the shows and determine if there are "crank" callers, slanted programming, or some other deterrent to your organization being there.

Good call-in shows, those that are well-managed, do provide a forum for your organization that you seldom get elsewhere. They also give you the opportunity to find out what is on the public's mind and that the public did not understand the issue you so carefully put before them.

Television talk shows cover both hard news and feature topics. Of special interest to television talk shows are subjects with visual support. Nothing is more dull than 30 minutes of a "talking head." Make the subject and the person interesting.

Television is also offering call-in shows on both local and national levels. Again, it takes a well-trained spokesperson who is willing to place himself or herself on the firing line for any potentially antagonistic caller.

The topics for talk shows are practically limitless and include standards of education, health care, consumer affairs, new technology, law, religion, business, minority affairs, energy conservation, sports, and personal finance.

One media relations staff in Chicago once helped a suburban radio station with three half-hour interviews with the company's business managers. The first segment discussed the company's community/education relations efforts as well as minority purchasing and affirmative action commitments. The second and third segments discussed jobs that will have a future in industry—what technical skills and educational backgrounds that industry will be looking for in future employees.

The messages were many, perhaps far too many for the print media, and there was not any real news value to the topics. There was, however, some interest, especially to the people who had never heard of the program and might be interested in employment in that company or industry.

LETTERS TO THE EDITOR

A letter to the editor intended for publication should not be written at each and every minor error, misquote, or suspected bias that appears in the paper. As with op-ed pieces, letters to the editor should be used judiciously.

Letters to the editor generally are in response to specific articles in the paper and can be used to clarify a point, rebut a charge, or simply react to a situation. Letters can also be used, however, to try to create interest in a subject that has not been covered by the media.

There is no guarantee your letter will be used, nor is there a guarantee that the letter, if used, will appear in a timely manner. Finally, there is no conclusive way to provide—to yourself or to your organization—evidence that the letter did any good.

If you decide you need to use a letter to the editor, it should adhere to certain guidelines. The letter should be short, directing its message only to one issue. It should never attack a reporter and it certainly should be factual.

Letters to the editor must be signed or they will not even be considered for publication. To make sure the editor and the reading audience understand the issue is of serious concern to your organization, have the letter signed by the chief executive officer, if possible. This is a stamp of credibility an editor would find difficult to ignore. It is also wise to check with the publication to see if there are additional criteria you must meet.

Remember, a letter to the editor to clarify a serious inaccuracy is welcome, for journalists are as concerned with accuracy and professionalism as you are. On the other hand, a letter written in spite or over a minor error appears juvenile and is treated with the same accord.

As with op-ed pieces, your letter to the editor should state the situation, give the background, and offer a solution to the problem or a change.

NEWS CONFERENCE

Just as a release has *news* as its adjective, so should a conference. After all, why should you call a conference if not to impart news to the media?

Unfortunately, the news conference has been badly mauled by publicity-seeking people or groups who offer little more than an orchestrated attempt to gain attention.

The news conference *should* offer both news and a forum for the exchange of information.

The first thing is to make sure your proposed announcement is worthy of the time and effort needed to produce a news conference. It will help if you ask yourself some questions:

1. Is this a major product announcement? (Remember, you can *announce* a product only once, after that, you *publicize* it.)
2. Is this announcement something that will have significant impact on the reading/viewing audience?
3. Is this a complex issue that cannot be explained with a release? Does the issue demand a forum so that reporters can ask questions?
4. Does the occasion involve a celebrity or major politician from whom the media would want quotes?

In short, always consider whether you can adequately give the information to the media via some other mechanism, be it news release, telephone conversation, briefing, or op-ed piece, before holding a news conference.

If you decide to conduct a news conference, you need to bargain for all the time and assistance you can get. A major product announcement should come only when all parties are ready to deal with the questions and demands that will result from the announcement.

The logistics of hosting a news conference are numerous. Questions must be answered concerning the location, the timing, who speaks when, who should be invited, should there be refreshments, and what material should be available.

Location. A news conference does not have to be held in the grand ballroom of the best hotel in town. Journalists will go to where the conference is if the event is worthy of the effort. A product announcement could be held in one of several places: manufacturing location, hotel, warehouse, trade conference site. Do not be tied down by the traditional; remember, journalists have to travel to where ribbon-cutting ceremonies and ground-breaking ceremonies are, so they will travel to your event if the event/news is worth it.

Wherever you hold the conference, make sure it meets the needs of the journalists. There should be room for cameras and there should be arrangements made for tables and chairs for all reporters. Make sure any power needs are met as well as any special lighting needs. Check the acoustics so that, if you have to, you can assist in setting up microphones for better coverage.

Time. Knowing your local media well means you will have no trouble determining when to hold a news conference. You should attempt to have the event at the best "down" time for all the media. More than likely, this will be during the late morning, after the television crews have been given assignments (one of which, you hope, is to cover your conference) and when there still is time for late-breaking news to go into the final afternoon edition of the newspaper. Reporters for the morning paper will be on duty, and radio reporters will not have yet completed the "heavy" newscasts for noon and late afternoon.

Check your community calendar to make sure you are not

conflicting with other major events, such as open houses, fairs, and demonstrations.

Notification. Alert the media a few days in advance, if at all possible. If you alert the media much before that, you take the chance of a leak. If you wait later than that, you may be too late in that reporters and camera crews will already have their assignments.

You may call the media to remind them of the conference but, if your first notification showed the importance of the conference, a reminder call can be misinterpreted as pushy.

Protocol. Each member of the media should be greeted when he or she arrives at the conference. They should be given press kits and shown the layout of the conference site, including where the camera crews should go and where print reporters can sit.

Start the press conference on time. Just as your speakers have other engagements, so do the media have other events to cover. Stay within the specified time for the announcement itself and try to not let the question-and-answer period linger beyond the point where questions become sparse.

Finally, thank the media for attending the conference. Do not assume they know you are grateful for their appearance.

Available Material. The press kit you offer to the media is critically important. The bulk of your preparations probably will center on this item; certainly, the bulk of your time will go into it.

The kit should have, besides the primary release reiterating what your spokesperson announced, other aids to help the media. If the announcement is a large, complex one, the kit may have several releases with each issue broken down into its component parts. It may have just the one release with a fact sheet to back it up. Depending on the situation, you may include photographs of your speakers, products, plants or services in the kit as well as 35mm color slides for television. You could have prepared actualities for the radio or a video clip for the television stations. Maybe you will need biographies of the speakers and/or copies of the speeches they give.

Each kit should be prepared to fit the event. Do not force the event to fit the kit.

Behind the scenes, you should have prepared all the questions and answers you and your staff could think of that might come up both at the conference and later after reporters have digested your material.

Emergency Conferences. Clearly, you need to hold a conference if there is a crisis which demands it, such as a bombing, a chemical scare, or a plant evacuation.

Equally clear is that you will not have the time to locate just the right place and prepare all the right materials and observe the minute details of decorum. In these cases, you operate under the rules of crisis management, which say that you have a plan to cover any eventuality that may occur. Your decisions will already have been made about details such as site, spokespersons, and protocol. (See Chapter 8.)

BACKGROUNDERS, BRIEFINGS, AND SEMINARS

Not all the tools for getting into the media involve instant returns. Therefore, as part of your ongoing relationships with editors and writers, you should consider having backgrounders, briefings, or seminars.

A backgrounder is a written piece that can be given to a writer or editor explaining the history of an issue, including how it came to be an issue in the first place. Often, background material is stated to be "off the record," a misnomer for something vital to the issue that should be *on* the record.

The backgrounder could be a compilation of news stories already written about the issue, technical papers, or even internal, nonproprietary reports that can be made available to the public.

A briefing, on the other hand, generally is a face-to-face proposition. Journalists are gathered to hear a speaker or speakers talk about an issue instead of trying to rely totally on written material in a backgrounder. A backgrounder package can stand on its own; a briefing package needs additional support, such as a backgrounder package.

Sometimes, a topic will be so complex that it requires a seminar to explain it. These can be held for specialty writers; for example, scientific writers, who need to have the issue, trend, service, technology, or theory explained in depth. Seminars should be conducted by the very best subject-matter experts you have.

NEWS FEATURES

An often overlooked tool is the news feature, a hybrid piece that combines the essence of news (after all, it is news if it meets the five-step criteria) and the style of feature writing.

News features are short articles written about aspects of your business or service operation which are interesting and informative but not necessarily "must have" news.

These features can describe unusual jobs or behind-the-scenes "how-to" operations or focus on one employee or volunteer. Smaller newspapers and magazines often are interested in these because they seldom have adequate staff to research and write their own features.

STAND-ALONE PHOTOGRAPHS

A photograph with a outline that succinctly describes the action in the picture can sometimes be more effective than a full press kit. Unusual photographs that still relay a message can meet both your objective and that of the photography editor to whom you send the item.

It should go without saying that only the finest photography should be considered for this avenue to the media. Whether it is a lucky on-location shot, or a carefully planned studio photograph, the final product should be able to stand by itself with just a short message in the cutline. Photos depicting technology, product usage, and milestones are a few of the types to be considered.

STAND-BY STATEMENTS/Qs AND As

If you know of an event that could break into the news and cause a reporter to call, there are two pieces of written information you might want to get working on just as quickly as possible. The first is a stand-by statement. This gives the basic facts of the situation and your organization's position. It is *not* a news release. Rather, it is a piece the spokesperson (the media relations person or whoever else is speaking publicly on this issue for your organization) will use to answer reporters' questions.

The second piece, Qs and As, is expected questions a reporter would ask you and the answers you will give if he or she does. Again, this is *not* material to be handed out to reporters, nor to be published in general employee information media. It is for use only to help you reply to questions from the reporters.

To be valuable tools, the stand-by statement and Qs and As should meet three basic criteria:

1. They should answer the five Ws that every reporter asks: who, what, where, when and why.
2. They should—as much as is possible—be cleared in advance so that you are ready to move quickly to answer a reporter's questions. The media's business is news, and a reporter's time frame is usually today. To get your organization's position in a story, you must meet the reporter's deadline. And you are almost always better off when your organization's view is included. In the absence of information, people "fill in"—often with the worst possible scenarios.
3. They should not be words that are cast in concrete. The spokesperson should not read the material verbatim but rather talk from the material.

The media relations tool kit is filled with items you can use both every day and others that are needed just every now and then. The trick is to know how to use each tool wisely and well.

———————

Test your use of the Media Relations Tool Box with these situations developed by David V. Manahan, Division Manager, Media Relations, AT&T Information Systems. For examples of how others have handled similar situations, see Chapter 7 and 8.

Your company introduces a new product that will not be available in your region for at least 6 months. How do you handle the PR? How can you position the company as a "live wire" organization without raising expectations? Without overhanging the market?

A reporter calls and wants confirmation of financial data on your company. It is obvious the reporter has figures from a recently held upper-management meeting but has interpreted some of them incorrectly. What do you do?

The San Francisco Examiner *is on deadline and needs a statement on the status of a new service offering from your organization. It is 5 P.M. in California and 8 P.M. in New Jersey. None of the eastern headquarters executives are at home. What do you do?*

There is a wildcat strike at a plant near Washington, D.C. The electronic media show up in force. How do you handle the situation?

A reporter calls you to do an interview with someone in your area on the deteriorating quality of service in your hospital. From your initial conversation with the reporter, you are sure that he has already written the story in his mind—and he is not going to say anything nice about the hospital. What do you do?

The Financial Times *of London calls to confirm rumors that your company is attempting to buy out a major European manufacturing concern. It is 11 A.M. in New York and 5 P.M. in London. Your executives are in meetings. What do you do?*

A reporter says he just got a call from a person who has just been laid off by your company. The reporter says the employee worked in a city that you know has identified a surplus situation. What do you do?

You have a product announcement, with a major press conference, scheduled for Wednesday. On Monday afternoon the business editor of a leading daily calls you and says he has all the details about your product, including its name. He is going to run something in Tuesday's edition. He just wants to confirm what he has. What do you do?

There is a major national trade show in your area. How do you work with the exhibits, product promotion, and marketing people to make this a media relations opportunity as well as a sales tool?

CHAPTER

4

REPORTERS

Helping them Meet their Objectives

The emphasis in a media relations program should be on the *relations* aspect—working to build long-term relationships with the people who cover your organization. Good media contacts proliferate once they are established. As is true with many good relationships, they are built only gradually, based on a variety of contacts over time, and strengthened by experiences that foster growing knowledge and respect. They require you to have a thorough understanding of how newspapers, magazines, and TV and radio stations operate on a day-to-day basis. But, in the end, this is a people-to-people business. A media relations person deals with writers, editors and photographers—not with newspapers, television stations and radio microphones. Knowing how to assist a reporter and his or her supporting cast will make the difference in long-term relationships with the media—the only kind to have.

DEADLINES ARE CRITICAL

The first thing to appreciate is that a reporter's life is controlled by very short deadlines. As *Time* publisher John A. Meyers put it: "Journalists are fond of the saying that they write the first draft of

43

history."[1] In every publication there is a "news hole" that must be filled by a predetermined time when the printing presses start running. At a daily newspaper that process occurs every 24 hours. Today's news must appear in today's paper—and tonight's news in tomorrow morning's editions. The reporter's success will be determined by how often his or her stories appear in the paper, rather than being "killed" (newspaper jargon is "spiked") by the editor. And if he writes a particularly interesting or difficult story, he will be rewarded with a byline—having his name appear over the story as the writer.

There are equivalent (and usually, more stringent) deadlines for electronic journalism. With the public demand increasing for frequent up-to-the-minute reports, the radio stations' past practice of carrying news only on the half-hour or hour and the TV stations' traditional two newscasts an evening are rapidly becoming obsolete. They are being replaced by numerous spot reports, lengthier regular newscasts, all-news programming on radio, and increasing numbers of 24-hour news formats on television (a true legacy of Ted Turner's Cable News Network). Because of the transitory nature of the airwaves, radio stations in particular usually repeat news reports several times. The broadcast journalist thus must meet more numerous and tighter deadlines than his print colleagues. Similar to publication bylines, the television journalist's reward for an unusually fine reporting job will be an appearance on camera to report the story in person; for a radio reporter it will be an actuality where the interview is carried on the air, rather than having the anchorperson or announcer simply read the story.

So two fundamental things are motivating the reporter: (a) the desire to report the story well; that is, accurately and in an interesting way and (b) the desire to write it quickly. To have the story used, the reporter must meet both requirements; to meet those demands *you* must meet the *same* criteria. A cogent statement or key fact is useless to the reporter today if it was needed as an integral part of yesterday's news story.

The first rule of good media relations, then, is to meet the reporter's deadline. This will usually demand that you respond the same day—frequently, within hours. That is easy to accept in theory, but in practice it often demands the time and authority to stop other work to devote your full attention to the reporter's needs until they are met. If clearances are necessary before you can release certain information, you also will need the influence to ask others to break into their routine to support you.

You should know the regular and late-breaking news deadlines of all the media which normally carry stories on your organization. Afternoon dailies, for example, usually "close" their inside pages about 9:30 in the morning and their front news pages about noon. Morning papers want all but major news material in by 2 or 3 P.M. the afternoon before. Some papers have editions going to different areas; if you are interested in a rural or suburban location, that edition may close a couple of hours earlier than the final or city edition. But these deadline times will differ depending on the distance between the paper's publishing plant and its circulation boundaries, and the time required to transport copies to the most distant subscriber or newsstand. Feature and Sunday sections close several hours, or even days, earlier. Weekly newspapers, which normally publish on Wednesdays or Thursdays, frequently have deadlines a few days before press day, except for major news stories.

The news desk of any publication or station will be happy to tell you its deadlines. You might want to phone those with whom you deal regularly, and then make a list of the deadlines which you can keep handy when you are working with reporters. In any case, it is a good habit to ask a reporter what his or her deadline is each time you get a request for information. This will ensure there are no misunderstandings between you, and let the reporter know you appreciate the importance of media deadlines. Over time you will come to a position of mutual understanding regarding deadlines: The reporter will learn he or she can trust you to do everything possible to meet deadlines, even the extremely short-fuse ones. In return, you will expect him or her not to "cry wolf" by creating artificial deadlines—and to give you additional time when the story is of a softer nature not demanding "today" treatment, or the request is for a large amount of information not readily available. If you cannot get all the information promptly, it often is wise to call the reporter to give an update on progress in case the story is being held for your input.

You will also want to avoid phoning a reporter around deadline time with anything but critical information related to that day's news. He or she will be busy writing, talking with the editor, checking last-minute facts, or working with the art department on the cutline for a photograph that will accompany the story—in short, getting the news out. There will be no time for chatting about a possible future feature story.

Attention to deadlines is also critical when you are issuing a news release or planning a news conference, because the hour you set as a release time almost inevitably favors some media over others. If you issue your news in the early morning, for example, the afternoon paper and evening TV newscasts will be the first to carry the news. If you schedule the release in the afternoon you are giving the opportunity for first coverage to the morning paper, and making it difficult for the evening TV news to carry anything but a brief mention unless they have the latest in portable camera/sound systems. As one TV reporter rebuked a reluctant spokesperson who asked if an on-camera interview could be delayed: "It's the 6 o'clock news, sir—not the six-forty. They'll be on the air with or without us."

The media in your particular area—and your analysis of the importance of each publication or station to your organization—will determine the time you schedule news releases and press conferences. A good general rule of thumb is to alternate between mornings and afternoons if you have both A.M. and P.M. papers in your area—or to always set news events and schedule release times to meet your weekly newspaper's deadline if it is the leading news publication in your community. Radio stations and teletext services that carry news report it just about instantaneously, or at the minimum every 60 minutes, and repeat it frequently. So the time you choose is not that critical to them.

If you are releasing copy for a public service announcement, you will want to pay even more attention to a station's or paper's deadlines, because you will not have the status of "real news" behind your request. Here again it would probably be worth your while to phone each outlet and make a list of the public service spot deadlines, because four-week lead times are not uncommon.

Another good rule of thumb is never to issue news releases or hold news conferences on Fridays unless you have no alternative. At best you could lose an opportunity to get your good news out to the widest possible audience, because Americans traditionally listen to fewer newscasts and read fewer newspapers on Saturdays than any other day of the week. At worst you could offend the press and make them think you are hiding something, if you are announcing bad news, because it will be more difficult for them to contact you after normal office hours. "You make a big announcement Friday afternoon and then go away for the weekend so I can't ask any questions," a reporter once said accusingly after a utility in Seattle had announced a major rate case. "It makes me think there's more to this than meets the eye."

The same prohibition applies to late afternoon announcements. Remember that good relations with the media often begin—not end—with a news release. You must allow reporters enough time to contact others about your story, ask questions of you and them, gather visuals to illustrate it, and generally adapt or rewrite your release to meet the interests of their particular audience.

Saturday, on the other hand, can be a good day for nonprofit organizations to issue news releases or hold news events. They will be covered on that evening's television news and in the next day's papers. Reading the bulging Sunday paper has become a day-long activity in many American cities. As well, you are less likely to have to compete for space with news of business, the stock market, the economy, the government, and other organizations that operate on Monday-to-Friday schedules.

Depending on the mail service in your area, and the release date and time for your news, you should consider either having people on your staff hand-carry your release to your normal contacts on the local papers and stations or hiring a delivery service. This will avoid the problem of your news arriving so late that it has lost its news value. It also will ensure that you get your news to all the media at about the same time, so you do not inadvertently help one reporter "scoop" another. You will want to address your envelope to a particular reporter or editor by name so it quickly gets to the right person—and perhaps also phone those who cover your beat regularly to tell them a release is on the way. If you are sending more than one copy to the same news outlet—for example, one to the assignment editor and one to the reporter who recently wrote a story about your organization—it is a courtesy to add a brief, handwritten note that says so. Be aware of any distribution idiosyncrasies at the publication or station. To cite an extreme example, if you fail to write "Personal and Confidential" over the addressee's name at The *Wall Street Journal*, the news release likely will be whisked away to the parent Dow Jones

News Service for distribution over its wire service. Thus your reporter may not get the news at all, much less by deadline time.

There are also many times when the confusion of last-minute deadlines can be avoided altogether. If your organization has an annual fund-raising event or is planning a major celebration like a fiftieth anniversary, you should write a letter several months in advance to the public service people if you will be requesting help with public service announcements, and a week or two in advance to the news editor if you think there are opportunities for straight news coverage. Even if you want to keep the nature of the news a secret until the event, a phone call advising a reporter you think he or she might want advance notice to keep the calendar clear on a certain day is the kind of thoughtfulness that helps build long-term personal relationships. A follow-up phone call the day before the news event is also a fine idea. Busy journalists are reminded of your event and you can get an idea of how many plan to attend. But do not overdo it by calling several times or pestering them for a definite RSVP. Even if an editor has assigned a news team to your event, late-breaking news could result in a last-minute change.

ACCESSIBILITY IS PARAMOUNT

On November 20, 1974, the media relations staff at AT&T's New York City headquarters had a luncheon honoring one of their number who was celebrating his fifteenth service anniversary. As was their normal practice, one staff member stayed behind to cover the office over the lunch period in case a reporter called with a request for information that could not wait. Also as a matter of routine, they left the name and phone number of the restaurant. In the middle of the luncheon the person covering the office answered a call from a reporter in Chicago who was phoning to find out why the New York Stock Exchange had suspended trading in AT&T stock. One call to the restaurant and everyone returned to the office to learn that the Department of Justice was about to file a major antitrust suit against the company. Within two hours AT&T was hosting a press conference to respond to the charges and answer questions on what became one of the biggest and most publicized cases in antitrust history—and resulted in the breakup of the Bell System 10 years later.

Holly Golightly opined in *Breakfast at Tiffanys,* "There are certain shades of limelight that ruin a girl's complexion." AT&T would not have wished for such a vivid example to demonstrate the value of its media relations administrative systems. But the fact remains that when an emergency hits and you are making instant history, there is no substitute for routine procedures already in place to ensure the accessibility of key spokespersons. They are crucial whether you work for a large, multinational corporation or staff a six-person office for a trade association.

As much as is practical you should match your office hours to the hours of the key media that cover your organization. If the main paper in your area is a morning publication, for example, its news reporters and key editors are much more likely to work from 10 A.M. to 6 P.M. than 9 to 5. Certainly you need a responsible person available throughout the luncheon period. If you have more than one person on your media relations staff, you may want to consider staggered hours to broaden your office coverage. If you work alone, an answering machine would be a wise investment. In any case, you need to set up a message system that helps you quickly get word of reporters' phone calls so that you can promptly return them. (We know of more than one case where people have waited several days to return a reporter's call—a discourtesy they would not inflict on their business associates, and one that forces the media to seek other sources within the organization.)

You should also have your home telephone number printed on your business card, and your office telex number if your organization has international operations or customers. Some people also include their home phone with their office number on every news release they issue. Reporters checking late-breaking news or calling from different times zones should always be able to reach you.

It is also extremely helpful to keep an up-to-date file of information about your company at your home. Your annual report, most recent financial results, latest organization chart, product catalogues and price lists—such information readily available at home will save your being embarrassed by appearing to be ignorant of basic facts about your organization. And make a regular practice of taking home every release you issue that day—plus backup information—in case someone calls you there after normal working hours.

Sometimes the topics will be too complex for you to feel comfortable handling without counsel from the person responsible for a specific area. Or sometimes a reporter will want to attribute the response to a high-level executive in your organization. Just as you want reporters to know how to get in touch with you after normal office hours, so you will want the residence phone numbers—and also vacation home numbers if they have them—of key executives or experts in your organization. You will also want those executives to be able to call you day or night if an emergency arises that might result in media attention; such as an injury to a worker in one of your facilities, a plane crash involving your employees, the death of a top executive, or a bomb scare. If your organization does not have such an emergency contact list, you may want to take the initiative by creating one, distributing copies to all employees involved for both their offices and homes, and then keeping it up to date. Be sure your main office switchboard operator has the list—but be certain all news media calls are referred to you first, day or night.

Many a time we have blessed the fact that reporters have our home numbers—and we in turn have the numbers of other key company people around the country. A significant case-in-point occurred in January 1982, a time when the recessionary economy was having a big impact on AT&T's equipment sales. The phone rang at home at 9:40 P.M. It was a reporter from the *Wall Street Journal*. He also was at home, and he was very apologetic. "I'm sorry to call so late," he said, "but some 'looney tune' just called the news desk in New York with a silly rumor that you are laying off 10,000 people and pulling out of the telephone manufacturing business. I know that's crazy, but they wanted me to check it out with you to see if there is any truth to it." As is the case with most crazy rumors, there was a grain of truth behind it. But this reporter knew our business well, so he immediately recognized that, at the minimum, the alleged news tip was highly exaggerated. Like the good reporter he is, he called to check.

We told him that indeed there was going to be a large layoff—1200 people, not 10,000—that the news would be told to employees beginning with the night shift in about an hour, and that the company would make a public announcement the next morning. We pointed out that the anonymous caller's statement that AT&T was pulling out of the telephone manufacturing business was not true, but unfortunately the declining demand for new home phones as a result of the current economic slowdown, especially in the housing market, was causing layoffs. We gave him some more details and then asked the key question: Did he plan to write a story? He replied that he thought he would.

If you read the *Wall Street Journal* the next morning, on January 6, you might have seen a relatively small 5- or 6-inch story on the layoff. But what you did not know about was the flurry of behind-the-scenes activity—both late that night and early the next morning—that the story caused. First and most important were the calls that night to our local public relations manager. We had to alert him to the leak, to the fact that there would be a story in the next day's *Wall Street Journal*, and we had to coordinate answers to some more of the reporter's questions. Also we wanted to let the PR manager and his staff know they had to move up their planned announcement to their local media. So they came in early and got their news release out at 7 the next morning. After all, it would not do much for their media relations if the local reporters read about a local layoff in the national *Wall Street Journal* before they heard it from our media relations people there. Also very important were our other major offices and plants around the country. We got a quick alert out to them very early the next morning, so they would be prepared to respond promptly and professionally to the inevitable calls they would get from reporters wanting to know the local situation. And we in New York got ready to handle the queries from other national publications, the wire services, and the trade press that we knew the *Journal* story would (and did) cause. It was a busy time. But there was never any confusion or concern about what to do or how to contact the right people even in the middle of the night. (The advance planning for the layoff announcement was also vital to the calm manner with which we were able to react to the leak; more about that in Chapter 8.)

KNOW THE NEWS PEOPLE AND THEIR MEDIA

Another important element in your relationship with the reporters who cover your organization should be your knowledge of their special interests—either because the publication or station has assigned them to the area or because they have a personal interest in the topic. Many times reading the bylined articles or columns of a print reporter, and listening to or viewing the programs of a radio or TV commentator will give you insight into subjects on which they seem to enjoy working.

If you think you have an idea for a feature, try to interest a reporter or an editor in doing it, rather than writing it yourself. Similarly, if you have a good photo opportunity, call the local paper or TV station assignment editor in the hope you can get a photographer or camera crew to come out. As *Time* publisher John Meyers put it, "Scratch a photojournalist and you will find a reporter who wields a camera instead of a typewriter."[2] Publications and stations are much more likely to use material they have spent their people's time developing. But never talk to two journalists on the same publication or station about the same story idea or event—for example, to both the education and business reporters about a high school job fair—without telling each that you have done so.

Don't be oversensitive to failure when you call with a news or feature idea. We unsuccessfully tried to interest the Associated Press national photo editor in two pictures before scoring with a unique shot of AT&T's 64K "computer on a chip" paired with a South American fire ant. That placement resulted in the company's high-technology message appearing in more than 200 publications, including *Newsweek*, the *Minneapolis Tribune, Nashville Tennessean, Baltimore Sun, Dallas Times–Herald* and *London Times*, with a circulation of more than 20 million in the U.S. and overseas. A few strikeouts are worth it if you hit a home-run like that every so often. Conversely, you will want to do at least a little research before you suggest story or photo ideas. It would be very embarrassing to recommend a program on controlling health care costs to a talk show host, only to be told they covered that topic last month.

As valuable as knowing the reporter's interests is understanding the role the publication or station has set for itself. The *Los Angeles Times*, for example, sees itself as a national newspaper. In fact, when airline deregulation resulted in fewer transcontinental flights leaving Los Angeles, the *Times* moved deadlines for one edition up 30 minutes so the paper could make the plane to Washington. "We want our paper on the desks of the President and Congress before they get to work in the morning," managing editor George Cotliar explained. "We want to have the same opportunity to influence discussion that the *New York Times* and the *Washington Post* have."[3] Knowing that strategy, you would probably decide to try to interest a *Los Angeles Times* editor in a subject related to a national issue like energy, and take an idea geared to a smaller community audience to a suburban paper instead.

If a newspaper is part of a chain like Gannett or Copley which has a news syndicate, or heads its own news service like the *Chicago Tribune* or *New York Times*, this association will also have some effect on an editor. He or she is likely to be more interested in stories affecting people or communities beyond the paper's own circulation boundaries. (Incidentally, reporters frequently are not told if their stories are picked up by the member papers when they have gone out over the news service or syndicate. You often can build some personal rapport with a reporter by forwarding copies of his or her stories that your clipping service picks up—especially if they are from out of state.)

If they carry news of more than employees' bowling scores and the company picnic, internal publications can also be effective, inexpensive tools to keep reporters informed about your organization and stimulate interest in feature stories. Some organizations include local media people on their mailing list for each issue of the company's employee newspaper or magazine. Others prefer to send only selected issues, with a business card or a note drawing the reporter's attention to a particular feature you think would be of interest. In any case, it is useful to remember that what we take for granted because we deal with it every day can be perceived as news by the local media—particularly if there is a local or human interest angle. Employees participating in Red Cross blood drives and the American Cancer Society "smokeout" days, features on car pools and other employee energy conservation ideas, suggestion program winners, tutoring activities with disadvantaged children, family nights at the plant, safety and handicraft fairs—all these are feature ideas we have placed with local media. Also, it is important for your management to recognize that once an issue is covered in your organization's employee media it can very easily get out. If a story appears internally, you should consider it externally released as well.

You will also want to have handy a standard package of materials about your organization to use as a backgrounder for

reporters doing stories on your company for the first time. The
annual report, a list of your key products and services, and a fact
sheet giving vital statistics such as number of employees, size and
features of your building, and contribution to the local economy in
terms of payroll, purchases, and taxes are the basics. You can then
add other information, depending on the thrust of the reporter's
story. Fact sheets need not be fancy—a plain typewritten sheet is
perfectly satisfactory. The important thing is that it be brief
(preferably no more than a page), current and carry the date on
which it was prepared.

HANDLING REQUESTS FOR INFORMATION

If you have an active media relations program, you are likely to get
calls from reporters almost every day. They may want more
information on a news release you issued. They could be working
on a feature story. Or they might want your organization's view on
a major news event of the day. There are, of course, a myriad of
ways in which you can respond to these queries. But one overall
rule applies: If you or your organization initiated interest in the
topic, you cannot duck or evade reporters' follow-up calls; if the
reporter originated the contact, your response will be dictated by
your company's objectives, policy and style.

    As you are working with people in your organization to write
and clear a news release, you will want to remind them that most
publications and stations will have their reporters call with additional questions rather than use the release as is. That is why you
should include anticipated media questions and agreed-upon
answers as a routine step in your advance planning and production
of any news release (see Chapter 3). You will want to ensure your
internal contacts are available on the day you issue the release—
and stay in your office yourself that day and probably also the
following one. You should also brief whoever answers your phone
on the importance of the release and the proper way to rapidly
handle the calls it generates. Reporters' normal sense of urgency
quickly turns to panic as their press or air time approaches. Believe
it or not, public relations people have actually issued news releases
and then gone into all-day meetings, leaving their secretaries alone
to fend off frustrated reporters seeking additional information.

On occasion you may also be called by reporters to get your organization's reaction to significant external news events, ranging from the announcement of a proposed change in federal tax policy to a local rezoning application for a new industrial park. Whether you are requested to comment on such general public issues will probably depend on the prominence of your organization within your community. Whether you choose to respond will often depend to a great extent on the personal style and civic involvement of your organization's top leaders. You should know or help establish your organization's general policy for handling such broad requests so that you can promptly deal with this type of media request. Follow your local media's coverage of such key issues so you can anticipate and plan responses for the types of calls you may get.

When a reporter asks for information, do not hesitate to ask enough questions yourself so you have a full understanding of the story on which the reporter is working. If you take a single, isolated question, you may not be able to give your expert enough to go on to offer a competent answer. Or the answer to the question, when relayed to the reporter, may lead to another question and you will have to go through the process all over again. Get a good grasp of what the reporter wants. Try to visualize the whole while you are talking about the parts. Anticipate followup questions. Be a reporter's reporter.

What you want to avoid is being perceived as a person intent on withholding information or, just as bad, a person who does not have access to information. There still remains a certain skepticism—and sometimes definite hostility—from journalists toward media relations people. The only way to overcome this is to prove yourself every time you work with the media. If reporters continually call direct to other sources within your organization, it is either because they do not know you or you are not meeting their information needs.

There is no sin in admitting you do not know an answer; simply say you will check it out and get back to the reporter. But if that happens very often, you should ask yourself some soul-searching questions:

1. Am I doing everything I can to keep current on company activities and industry trends? Should I expand my regular

reading? Make a point of keeping in touch with people in
other departments? Be more active in trade associations or
professional societies?

2. Am I anticipating news and activities in this organization
   that would cause media interest, and preparing to handle
   news queries in advance?

3. Am I—or is my boss—included in planning meetings and
   the decision-making process? Do I have the confidence of
   top management so that I am among the first to know what
   is happening within the organization? (If not, you cannot
   be considered a spokesperson; at best you may be a
   well-qualified reference point.)

Recently, a fellow media relations practitioner complained
vociferously that he was left out of the planning and media
announcement activities when his company was awarded a major
government contract in a bid against the Japanese. But even
superficial questioning made it clear he had not kept up with the
current highly sensitive government negotiations on lowering
foreign import barriers. Nor was he aware of the various Congressional committees conducting hearings on international competition at the time. And he was not a regular reader of the trade press
covering his industry. So he was never up to date on what his
company's competitors were doing, nor how the industry viewed
his company. Little wonder his boss—and perhaps his CEO—felt
that he was not qualified to be the company's spokesperson on this
critical subject.

Similarly, watch to see what happens to your news releases.
You will soon come to accept the fact that reporters will rewrite
your carefully crafted sentences. If they do it too often, however,
you might ask yourself why. Are you following the accepted rules
of press style? (The *New York Times*, Associated Press, United
Press International, Ayer, or another widely accepted style book is
a must to be kept handy as a constant reference source.) Or maybe
the reporter's sentences are shorter and easier to understand than
yours. It is critical that news releases and statements be written in
plain English; not in "legalese," and not in corporate gob-
bledeygook. You may feel this point is so basic as to be unnecessary. Unfortunately, our experience has not shown that to be the
case. But if it is true, as an AT&T advertising campaign once told

us, that to communicate is the beginning of understanding, surely it must also be true that we must all comprehend the terminology.

SPEAK IN PLAIN ENGLISH

A reporter is a lot more likely to get your position right—or indeed, use your statement at all—if it is a "quotable quote." Similarly, the public is a lot more likely to agree with you if you speak in terms they can understand. Multisyllable words and diplomatic nuances prompted language expert William Safire to coin the term "Haigspeak" and quote comedian Mark Russell: "Who would have thought, between Secretaries of State Henry Kissinger and Alexander Haig, the one with the accent would be the one we can understand?"[4] Organizations bring much of the public's misunderstanding and mistrust upon themselves when they issue news releases and statements full of highly technical jargon and industry lingo. You can get so lost as you read or listen to so-called information sources that you don't know if you have been eating magic mushrooms or wandering around Alice's Wonderland. As AT&T Bell Laboratories President Ian Ross put it: "As we enter the Information Age, it would be ironic if we should fall prey to an information gap."[5] This could happen if we have not adequately defined our terms.

Mark Twain said that writers should strike out every third word on principle: "You have no idea what vigor it adds to your style."[6] United Press International sent out what it termed a "war on verbiage" message to all of its news bureaus: "Fight the battle sentence by sentence, paragraph by paragraph," the advisory said. "The result will be a sharply angled, concise news story that will deserve every inch of newspaper space it gets. The most effective weapon in the battle to achieve tighter writing is good reporting. Inevitably, the less we know the more we write."[7] All media relations people would do well not only to help reporters follow these guidelines but also adapt them for our own.

Never give away an "exclusive." If a newspaper, radio or TV station develops a feature article on its own and comes to you for information, or is approaching a news story from a unique angle, its rights to exclusive use of that story must be respected. If two reporters seek the same information, however, tell each person that the other is working on the story. It will avoid subsequent conflict and help keep you from being caught in the middle.

HANDLING REQUESTS FOR INTERVIEWS

Many times reporters will call an organization asking to interview someone about a particular topic. The natural reaction is to try to find an appropriate person for the reporter to talk to—sometimes a time-consuming and unnecessary effort. Often, a better response is for the media relations spokesperson to be the primary source of information for the majority of requests, reserving the interview for occasions when a person from another field is needed for his or her particular expertise or when the medium warrants an executive-level spokesperson. Having the media relations person be the primary spokesperson will probably mean your organization responds more promptly and more efficiently to reporter inquiries.

When you determine an interview with someone else is the best approach, however, there are a number of steps to follow. This section will deal with your support of the reporter in an interview situation. Chapter 5 will cover your work with your organization spokesperson.

The first decision is whether the interview will take place on the phone or in person. It is a good idea to ask the preference of the reporter. Radio or overseas reporters normally want a telephone interview because it is so much faster. Print or TV reporters' choices are usually determined by their deadlines and distance from your interviewee. But equally important is your input into the decision, which should be based on your knowledge of the spokesperson's desires and abilities in different situations, and your evaluation of the significance of this particular medium and story. If your spokesperson is just one of many sources to be interviewed for a broad survey article in a newspaper or magazine, for example, a phone conversation is probably most appropriate. Telephone interviews are usually shorter because there is less tendency to chitchat. If your organization is to be featured more prominently in the piece—be it in print or on TV—a face-to-face interview is probably best. Your spokesperson is more likely to come across as a personable human being rather than a faceless bureaucrat. But you will want to exert some control over the length of the interview and prevent it from dragging on unnecessarily.

Regardless of which medium is chosen, you should immediately provide the reporter with a biography—and a photograph, if one is readily available—of your spokesperson so he or she has a brief prior "introduction" to the subject. This is also the time to point out how the spokesperson prefers to be addressed, in person and in print; the correct spelling and pronunciation of the name, if it is unusual; and the person's particular field of expertise vis-à-vis the story the reporter is writing. Whenever possible you should provide this personal information, along with other appropriate background on your organization and the subject of the proposed story, in advance of the interview—even if this requires your having the material delivered by hand. The more you communicate with and provide background to reporters before the interview, the more they are likely to get the facts straight and not waste their and your spokesperson's time with basic "How does it work?" or "What does your company do?" questions.

If you have agreed on a phone interview, let the reporter know you will initiate the call at the agreed-upon time. Elementary as this may sound, double-check the time if different time zones are involved—especially with an overseas reporter. Because many people object to speakerphones, feeling their words are being broadcast all over, it is often best to set up a three-way conference call. After introducing the reporter to the spokesperson, let the reporter take control of the conversation. You, meanwhile, should take extensive notes of the conversation—verbatim if you can write quickly enough. Neatness definitely does *not* count when it comes to these notes. The only person who needs to be able to read them is you, so that you can check a quote for the reporter if you are requested to do so, or check the resultant piece for accuracy. If you are dealing with a particularly sensitive subject, however, you may want to write up your notes, including key questions and answers, for your files in case there are questions later about what was said or done. As you monitor the conversation, make notations to yourself if you feel points need clarifying or further data need to be gathered. Resist the urge to intrude on the conversation unless your spokesperson is stumbling and clearly needs you to help with an explanation, or is in danger of giving out proprietary or other sensitive information in response to the reporter's question or prodding.

If the interview is in person, arrange to meet with the reporter a few minutes in advance. Then you can briefly get acquainted if you do not already know the reporter, and review plans before you go to your spokesperson's office. After making introductions you should again avoid getting involved very deeply in the conversation. Take notes and offer counsel and follow up where necessary. You should also politely end the interview if the reporter's questions become repetitious, or if the time has extended much longer than originally scheduled to a point you feel to be inappropriate. It is rare for an interview to be profitable to both parties if it lasts much longer than an hour.

If a still photographer is accompanying the reporter for shots of the interview, there should not be much extra coordination required on your part beyond alerting your spokesperson. But if you know the photographer wants to tour your operation to take additional photographs, and you have the staff available, you should stay with the reporter and get someone else to work with the photographer and take care of critical details like photo permissions, safety, and security concerns. If a TV station wants to send in a camera crew, you should make sure the room where the interview will take place does not have too many windows, or a busy or strongly patterned background. Check the crew's space, lighting and electricity requirements in advance. Portable battery belts and hand-held TV cameras (called "mini-cams" because of their small size) are making the horror story of popping circuit breakers in the executive suite a thing of the past. But the addition of a crew—a cameraperson, (probably) an audio engineer and (maybe also) a lighting expert—means added distraction and tension for your spokesperson, and requires special attention on your part (see Chapter 5).

After the interview, get the reporter's deadline for any additional data you agreed to provide, and ask for a general idea when the story is expected to run. (No reporter can promise a publication or air date. That prerogative is reserved for editors.) Offer to check quotes or verify any additional information needed as the article is being written—a polite way of letting the reporter know you care about accuracy but understand you cannot see the copy in advance.

Once the story appears, if you feel it was a difficult subject handled well or written in a particular interesting way, you should not hesitate to tell the reporter either in a phone call or the next time you meet in person. Like all of us, reporters are interested in honest feedback and flattered by positive reactions. If the story does not appear within the expected time frame, it is acceptable to phone the reporter check the status—as long as you make clear your understanding that editors make these decisions, not reporters. If the story is "killed"—a term newspaper reporters use when a story is written but never printed—you must not protest too strongly. It is fine to inquire as to the reason, because you may learn from it and thus improve your media relations in the future. But most stories do not appear for the simple reason that news is plentiful, space is limited and editors must make judgments on the value of each story.

HOW TO HANDLE ERRORS

The news media have neither the space nor the time to tell the "whole truth." Rather, they carry the part their reporters think important. Under pressures of time and without detailed knowledge of your business, it is inevitable that errors will occasionally appear in news coverage of your organization. Your behavior in this situation will have a major effect on your long-term relationship with the reporter and the publication or station. A natural first reaction is to demand a correction or write a letter to the editor. But that should more properly be a last resort, because the publication of a retraction, like a double-edged sword, cuts both ways. Errors read but once may be quickly forgotten; read twice, they may stick despite the attempt at correction.

Whether you are approaching the print or electronic media about an error, you will be dealing with a person who can naturally be expected to be defensive if he or she wrote or photographed the offending piece, or protective if he or she is the editor of the person under attack.

Here, in order of consideration and seriousness, is what you should do if there is an error in print coverage of your organization.

1. In most cases be charitable and do nothing. Most errors are insignificant in the context of the overall story. They will probably

not be noticed by any but the most knowledgeable in the audience, who would recognize that there was a mistake anyway. Sometimes it is the headline that offends. Remember that it is written not by the reporter but by a copy editor under incredible space constraints to summarize the essence of the story in a few words. With such brevity can come obscurity or misplaced emphasis. You should not blame the reporter, who probably did not see the headline before the piece was published or aired.

2. In some cases contact the reporter to request the item be corrected in the "morgue" (newspaper jargon for the file room or library where old issues are clipped and catalogued for future reporters' background use). Your purpose here is to politely alert the reporter to the error and ensure it is not repeated in future coverage of your organization. An example of a mistake warranting a correction in the file copy might be a misstatement about your product line or the size of your facility, or a name misspelling or incorrect title of one of your executives. A particularly clever complaint letter was sent by AT&T media relations spokesperson Wink Swain to a reporter who got her companies mixed up: "Oops! As much as I enjoyed (name of reporter's) article on Westinghouse Broadcasting, I'm afraid there was a slight error in corporate genealogy. Western Electric is not the parent company of Group W, though the article was so well done that I almost wish we were," the letter said. "Western Electric is a wholly owned subsidiary of AT&T.

"The enclosed booklet will tell you all about us. We're certain that the error was innocent, and we don't want to make a big fuss over it. I hope that you and (name of reporter) will accept the friendly reminders that I've enclosed and use them to serve the people of (the town)." Along with a booklet describing the company, Swain sent two pens carrying the corporate logo. The morgue was corrected and a mistake was turned into a friendly media contact.

3. In a few cases you will want to write a letter to the editor. This can be done when you feel your position was not adequately stated—as compared to being incorrectly stated—and you want to use the forum of the Letters to the Editor column to expand exposure of your views. Or it might be appropriate when you want to publicly and formally correct the record, as when your organization is involved in a legal or regulatory action.

4. In rare cases you will be justified in asking the publication to print a correction. This would occur, for example, if your earnings or other pertinent financial information affecting the price of your stock were misquoted. Or sometimes a correction can be masked by the addition of updated information; for example, including the time and place of the funeral in a second article when the person's name was misspelled in the initial obituary.

5. In no case should you contact the competing paper to tell them of the incident and ask them to set the record straight. Ethical journalists will not participate in vendettas against their colleagues.

The last item in the list applies to radio and TV as well. Do not call competing stations and ask them to carry the "true story."

There are differences, however, when you are dealing with the broadcast media instead of print. If you call up a radio station to complain of an error in coverage, the station often will ask your permission to tape you over the phone then and there, giving your side of the story. They may use your comments live if the program is a talk show with a call-in format. Or they may save the tape for a later broadcast. Before you call you will want to be prepared with two or three key points written down to help you state your position coherently. A TV station could also ask you to appear on a guest editorial giving your position if the issue is controversial or of long-term significance to your community.

You, of course, must be even more swift in correcting any errors that go out in your materials to the print or broadcast media. No matter how careful you are, one day an error is going to slip through your checking and proofreading system. If it is clearly only a typographical error, there is no need to issue a correction and a second release—although you will want to redouble your proofing efforts because even small errors reflect on your professionalism and desire for accuracy. But if it is a significant mistake—a name misspelled or a factual error—you must *immediately* get on the phone to everyone to whom you sent the release, offer a quick apology, and give the correct information. Then you should also send out a revised news release to everyone on the original distribution list, with the words "corrected version" prominently written on the top of the first page.

WHEN TO SAY NO

In spite of the fact that your major role for reporters is to facilitate access to data and people in your organization, there are legitimate reasons for you to refuse to divulge information. There is, however, no occasion we have ever run across when it is appropriate for you or any spokesperson for your organization to reply to a media query with a terse "No comment." That is a desperate response, almost guaranteed to make the reporter search for other sources for the facts.

Better is to tell the reporter *why* you can't discuss an issue in much detail—because it involves proprietary information that will divulge too much to your competitors, because you are in the midst of sensitive labor negotiations and want to keep discussion going around the bargaining table rather than on the pages of the daily newspaper, because it is too soon after the accident to know what actually happened, because your lawyers have not yet received the court papers, or whatever is appropriate (see Chapter 6). The reporter then has a legitimate quote from you, and yet you have released no inappropriate information to the public. Both the media's and your organization's objectives have been met. (By the way, when you are citing proprietary information as the reason for refusing to disclose information, you want to be sure it really *is* proprietary. One spokesperson refused to acknowledge the existence of a new manufacturing process, only to have the reporter pull out a company brochure with a photo of the alleged secret equipment. On another occasion a media relations person refused to divulge the salary of the CEO and president until caustically reminded by a reporter that the figures were carried in the company's legally required public reporting to the Securities and Exchange Commission as well as the annual meeting mailing to shareowners.)

On some occasions you may decide to say no to a reporter's request because of the time it would take to gather the information, or because the information is not available in the form the reporter wishes. These types of requests often come from editors or reporters seeking to localize news of a regional or national company by breaking down sales or financial information at the local manufacturing or sales office level. In these cases a simple statement that it would be too costly for your organization to keep statistics in every conceivable format, combined with an offer of the information in a somewhat different arrangement, is usually sufficient.

There are also situations when reporters do not seem to know what they want. When we come upon a writer whose questions and requests for information indicate a fishing expedition rather than a story, we politely but firmly ask him or her to determine the focus of the piece, at which time we will be pleased to help.

In extreme cases you might want to decline a guest appearance on a TV interview or radio talk show. For example, if the host has a record of asking loaded questions ("Do you still beat your wife?") or espousing positions contrary to your organization, industry or issue, your appearance may provide only a target for complaints rather than a forum for discussion. If a fellow guest is a bitter ex-employee or vocal union leader complaining of working conditions, your appearance could tend to legitimize the complaint and hurt relationships with your current employees. If the theme of the coverage is not supportive of your objectives—the favorite recipes of a woman candidate for senator, for example—a polite no may also be the best response. Sometimes no publicity is better than frivolous publicity.

Other legitimate times to say no may be those rare occasions when you cannot confirm that a free-lance writer or photographer is actually on assignment for a publication or station. If you are not familiar with a person who says he or she works for the media, it is a good practice to call the news desk or assignment editor of the appropriate medium to verify the assignment. The editor in charge will be happy to take your call; no publication or station wants unaffiliated people posing as their staff reporters or "stringers" (writers in smaller markets who occasionally are assigned news stories and features for a large publication).

There may be rare situations when you or your organization have dealt with a particular reporter on several occasions and believe he or she has such a bias or is so careless that almost all the resultant stories have been negative or inaccurate. A businesslike but candid discussion with the reporter's editor—in person rather than on the phone—will usually result in another person's being assigned to do stories on you if your complaint is deemed valid by the editor. But this is a last-resort action that should be taken only in exceptional cases when your allegations are well documented.

Editors tend to be defensive of their reporters and profession, especially when criticized by the subject of an article.

POTPOURRI

Here are some miscellaneous hints to help you anticipate, and thus be prepared to promptly respond to, reporters' requests:

1. When you are issuing a news release on an executive speech, make copies of the full text to have handy in case a reporter asks for it. The request may be caused by the reporter's desire to rewrite or expand on your news release. Or, the reporter may want to file the talk for use as background or source material in future stories. In any case, your anticipating such requests will enable you to get the speaker's agreement in advance to release the full speech—which can be annotated, if necessary, with the phrase "as prepared" or "as delivered" if there are or could be changes to the typed text. It is also a good idea to have copies of the speaker's biography and photo available to send out to those publications which regularly use photos.

2. Documents filed with a government regulatory agency such as the Securities and Exchange Commission or at a courthouse as part of a trial automatically become part of the public record. You can save the reporter some trouble, buy your organization goodwill, and help assure that your position is accurately carried in the story by copying an extra set of such filings if a reporter requests it.

3. Set up a file of biographies and photographs of your organization's key officers, managers and board members. You can create a standard form to be filled out and used as is. Or, you can write up a one-page narrative based on that information. Ask for each person's community newspapers if you live in a large metropolitan area; sometimes news of your managers appearing in their local paper means more to the family than coverage in a big city newspaper. Update the biographical data whenever there is a job change, or every 2 years. Photos should be $5'' \times 7''$ or $8'' \times 10''$ black-and-white formal studio shots, with new ones taken every 5 years at a minimum. You may also want to include some candid photos of your top executives—and some color slides if you expect

TV coverage, but remember that all television graphics must be 1¼ times wider than they are high to properly fill the screen.

REMEMBER YOUR ORGANIZATION'S EMPLOYEES

Your desire to be responsive to reporters' information requests cannot supersede your responsibility to the employees of your organization. When you are making an announcement to the external media, you will want to coordinate the release time with whoever is responsible for internal communications so your employees do not read news of your organization in the local paper before they learn of it at work. When there is an external leak ahead of the planned announcement time, you should immediately alert the employee communications person so a decision to advance the internal release can be considered. (Your colleagues should be equally considerate of you, and provide advance copies of all employee communications materials so you are aware of what is covered in case they get into reporters' hands.)

When you know media coverage affecting your organization is going to appear, you should also alert your internal communications person. If a positive piece is expected—for example, a feature on one of your workers or an interview with your CEO—your employees will appreciate knowing in advance, especially if it is on radio or television, so they do not miss it. If a negative piece is upcoming, you will want to ensure that employees have your organization's position on the topic in case they get questions from their family and friends.

If the media coverage is significant enough, you should also consider an advance alert via phone or letter to your organization's board of directors or trustees, key customers, or contributors—and perhaps also send them a representative sample of clipping or a transcript after the event.

---

*Here is some advice on how media relations people can do a
better job of meeting the media's needs:*

"If you become acquainted with representatives of the media
and stay in touch, it will reap rewards for your organization. Pick
up the phone and say, 'I'm so and so. I work for this organization. I
wanted you to know who I was, so if you have questions about what
we do out here, you'll know who to call.' Follow that up with a letter
saying, 'I talked to you on the phone. Here's what you need to know
in the way of phone numbers day and night.' Include a suggestion
for a story. Say, for example, 'You may be interested to know that
we just started making widgets along with fidgets, and it might make
a story for you.' Look around for an interesting employee who
would make a good feature article or profile—a fellow who in his off
hours collects antique telephones, for example. Someone who would
be interesting to the public, since that's who we represent you to.
Then stay in touch with the media. Make sure they know you're on
the scene and ready to help if they have an inquiry."

—Dave Beeder, Business Editor
Omaha World-Herald

The best type of PR person is the one who is receptive when we
call—who is willing to tell the company side of the story in bad
situations and good. If the company comes forward with whatever
they can say about what's happening, then the news media will
report that. We are looking for information. We want to know your
side of any story. I think the fairest reporting will come when a PR
person is helpful and informative when the news is bad as well as
good.

—Jim Scott, Assignment Editor
WISH-TV, Indianapolis

"We like the hard news, of course—a change in employment or
a new product announcement, for example. But we also like little
features—a photo of an employee blood drive or a story on a shop
crew building a special tricycle for a handicapped girl. Every one
that is brought to us will not make the paper, but we like to take a
look at them and see."

—Carey Cameron, Business Reporter
Gwinnett [Georgia] Daily News

Never lie. If you don't want to answer the question, just say so. If you say, "I can't give you that information right now," I can accept that. I might not be happy as a reporter or an editor, but it won't make me lose my trust. People appreciate realness. If you are accessible . . . if you are open and honest . . . if you say, "Here's what I think and here's why," people will respect you and your organization whether or not they agree with your position.

—Dan Warner, Editor
Eagle Tribune *(North Andover, Mass.)*

Return phone calls from reporters immediately. It will make them love you. Do this even if you have nothing to report. If you are waiting for an executive or source to return your call, tell this to your reporter contact, who will understand and value the feedback on the status of the inquiry.

—Tim Padmore, Business Editor
The Sun, *Vancouver, Canada*

Establish a relationship with one reporter at each station or publication. Over time, if you always are honest and straight, rapport will become trust. Then, when a mistake is made, it should be admitted. It hurts an organization more to hem and haw than to come right out and say 'We made a mistake.' The media will be understanding if you are honest. We only attack when you won't admit you made a mistake.

—Bobby Batiste, Anchor
CNN Headline News

What journalists are always after is news. What you want us to cover is propaganda. A good public relations person finds the middle road and meets the journalist half way. Remember also that reporters are always under time pressure. We need to know what's happening today and what will happen tomorrow—and we usually need to know it now. Your value depends on meeting our deadline.

—Frederick Ungeheuer, Financial Correspondent
Time

5 SPOKESPERSONS

Training and Briefing Them for their Role

In Joseph Heller's book *Good as Gold,* the hero is invited to go to Washington and be a "reliable source." If he is good at it, he is told, he will be promoted to being a spokesman.[1] It is true that performing effectively as a public spokesperson often brings accolades from within and outside the organization. But, as with all high-risk, high-reward situations, there are pitfalls.

When you are dealing with the media, any mistake is liable to be a very public one. Visions of a terrible *faux pas* splashed across the pages of the local newspaper or appearing on television screens in countless living rooms throughout the community tend to make our stomachs churn. Indeed, *The Book of Lists* ranks fear of public speaking ahead of death, flying, and loneliness[2]—and talking with a reporter for attribution has to be the most public of public-speaking opportunities. No wonder people in our organizations react with something approaching terror at the thought of a media interview, especially on a sensitive subject.

An anecdote cited in journalism circles tells of a city editor who called a reporter to the city desk to point out a mistake in a story. "Well," he said, "you have already made two-hundred-eighty thousand mistakes today and it is only noon." That "two-hundred-eighty thousand" was the paper's circulation figure. The comment impressed the reporter, and it should impress a spokesperson.

Like so many other talents, the skills required to be an effective spokesperson can be practiced and perfected. That associate whom you admire for the apparently natural ability to speak with clarity and charm undoubtedly is as nervous as you are. But training and experience have helped him or her to master fear—or at least mask it. John O'Toole, chairman of the board of the Foote, Cone & Belding advertising agency, pointed out in his book, *The Trouble with Advertising*...: "No matter what you do in life, your success at it relies heavily on your ability to communicate and explain your point of view to others in a way that will convince them to share it, or at least consider sharing it. This is called persuasion, and every human being is engaged in it constantly."[3]

A vital part of your job in media relations is your ability to be proficient enough in interview techniques and knowledgeable enough of the organization's policies and products that you can help your spokespersons prepare for news media contacts. At best this training should be part of an ongoing program. At the minimum it should be included as part of the routine briefing session you have with your spokesperson before any media interview.

CHOOSING A SPOKESPERSON

Before discussing the support of spokespersons, it is well to step back and talk about selecting the right one. The choice is not as obvious nor as easy as many people think. Indeed, it is one of the critical elements that will determine the success of your media coverage.

First of all, the obvious and frequent choice—the chief executive officer of your company or organization—is not always the best one. CEOs deal with broad, general, policymaking matters. Rarely are they involved in the nitty-gritty of the organization enough to know the details of a specific project or issue. Unless your CEO has a personal desire to be the primary spokesperson, you are better off reserving access to the top for reporters whose article requires comments on overall policy or strategic direction.

Nor is the head of the department involved in the topic

necessarily the right person. Promotions in organizations are normally based on outstanding technical or professional knowledge and performance. Department heads may have the ability to make a presentation at an internal meeting or to the board of directors, but this is not quite the same as being able to meet with reporters. When and if the spokesperson is chosen from a middle or lower echelon, be mindful of the sensitivities of that person's superiors in the organization. The top manager is usually known as such in the community. Do not make it look as if someone has usurped the leadership.

The sex or age of the person usually is not relevant to the decision. Some claim that a middle-aged man is a better choice because he projects authority. Others point to a 1981 Boston University study showing that women are more trusted than men, and thus make better public spokespersons, particularly in government, where there was a dramatic difference in trust of male and female spokespersons in similar positions.[4] Our advice is simply to pick the person who can do the best job.

As the media relations person, you should become familiar with the abilities of others in your organization so you can choose the best spokesperson for each media opportunity. Here are the characteristics you are looking for:

1. Above all, knowledge of the topic to be discussed with the reporter. Only with a firm grounding in the facts can anyone speak confidently and positively.

2. An understanding of the organization's overall objectives and strategies. There is no way every one of the reporter's questions can be anticipated. You want someone who can think quickly and also gracefully walk the fine line between being responsive to the reporter's needs and "giving away the store."

3. An ability to tell and sell what he or she knows—in everyday English and from the point of view of the reporter and the publication's or station's *audience*.

4. The confidence of top management. This person will be representing your organization to the general public. You do not want to choose someone who is not well respected by those within.

5. A desire to do the interview. If your proposed spokesperson demurs beyond what normal modesty and apprehension would explain, you probably should drop your

request. People tend to be honest with themselves; you should take heed when people believe they are poor choices for the assignment. There is a world of difference between being named a spokesperson and serving as one.

PREPARING YOUR SPOKESPERSON

Once you have determined who will be your organization's spokesperson for a particular interview, there is a great deal the media relations person can do to support the one who has accepted this sensitive and important assignment. The fact that many of the steps with your spokesperson parallel those you are taking with the reporter is no coincidence. Indeed, your role as the bridge between the media and your organization is amply tested in an interview situation. Whether you perform valuable service to both parties or are perceived to be an unnecessary third person by either depends on your professionalism. The quality of your work will be reflected both in the resultant media coverage and in that spokesperson's response to your future requests to talk with reporters.

Immediately after you have set the appointment and determined whether the interview will be on the phone or in person, you should communicate with your spokesperson. Whether you do so in person or by writing a memorandum does not matter. What is important is that your message to the spokesperson contains the following information:

1. Date, time, place and expected length of interview. If this is a new experience for this person, state that you will attend the in-person interview or set up the phone interview, depending which it is, to take notes and get any follow-up information needed by the reporter.

2. Type of story the reporter is working on—in-depth feature on your organization or survey piece on your industry, for example. Has the reporter's conversation already indicated a clear point of view for the story? Or is he or she doing an overview piece and searching for a local angle?

3. What the reporter told you he or she wants from the interview—quotes on your corporate objectives, general sales

plans for a new product line, your organization's opinion of a new community development plan, or whatever.

4. What you have provided the reporter. Describe briefly what information you have given the reporter during your phone conversations. List the materials you sent the reporter as part of the background package (see Chapter 4), and include them as attachments to the memo or go over them in person if you think the spokesperson might not be familiar with them. Your objective here is to let the spokesperson know what has already been said to the reporter so he or she can expand on it rather than merely repeat it.

5. Background on the reporter if this is the first time the spokesperson has dealt with this particular journalist. Does the reporter regularly write stories on your organization, or is this a first? Does he or she understand your business, or will the spokesperson have to be especially careful to explain the terminology? What has been your experience with the reporter in earlier contacts? Does he or she take notes or use a tape recorder? (You should welcome the use of a tape recorder, since it ensures accurate quotes.) It is a good idea to include samples of the reporter's recent stories—or suggest the spokesperson tune in to the appropriate program if it is a TV or radio interview and you have enough advance notice. This is particularly important for talk shows like ABC's "Good Morning America," NBC's "Today," PBS's "MacNeil-Lehrer Report," or their local equivalents, because journalists' interviewing styles can vary widely.

6. If photography is involved, any special arrangements you are making for the photographer or television crew. Explain the set-up time required for TV production equipment, especially if the interview is taking place in the spokesperson's office—or arrange to move the interview to another office.

7. Suggestions of two or three key points you think the spokesperson should stress in the interview. Here is where you make your greatest contribution, not only as a media relations professional but also as a counselor to your organization.

8. Advice on key interview techniques. (See following section, "Hints on Interview Techniques" for a full review of such advice. It is presented as a unit so that you can easily use all or part of the section when working with your spokesperson.)

9. Offer—no, *insist* on the need—to get together to review

anticipated questions and possible answers before the actual interview. (If it is a televised interview in the spokesperson's office, the time the crew takes to set up lights and other equipment provides a fine opportunity for you to get away from the turmoil for a discussion.) This initial backgrounding is important. If the interview is two or three days hence, it helps the spokesperson focus thoughts and prepare responses. If, as is so frequently the case, the interview is later that same day or early the next, it provides a framework in which to operate. It also means your briefing session just before the interview is likely to be more productive; that is, more concerned with content than logistics.

HINTS ON INTERVIEW TECHNIQUES

Most reporters are far too sophisticated to be impressed by style over substance. Conversely, a fine position can be misunderstood if it is not presented with clarity and confidence. Interviews are not conversations—they are highly structured situations. Some of television's top news people support your becoming more skilled in interview techniques. "It makes perfect sense to me because people should have every opportunity to make the best case they can for themselves," Mike Wallace told the *Washington Journalism Review*.[5] And John Chancellor added, "It's okay to bone-up for an interview as long as it teaches one not to hide the facts."[6] David Brinkley, questioned by the same publication on his views of spokespersons rehearsing for media interviews, replied: "It's about time they did. . . . They are dealing with the American people through us. . . . They give short, clear answers because they're more effective when they are delivered by us to the American people. I think that is a positive development and I would say it took them long enough to learn."[7] Similar thoughts were voiced by Irving Shapiro, retired chairman of duPont and also a chief spokesperson for corporate America by virtue of his heading Business Roundtable, the organization of CEOs of major industrial companies, in the mid-1970s: "You wouldn't drive a car without practicing, and when you go into the world of professional TV you ought to know what the experience is like. If you don't know that, you're at a huge disadvantage."[8]

Here are some interview techniques that should help you do a better job when you are interviewed by a reporter.

Prepare and practice. Mark Twain once said it takes 3 weeks to prepare a good ad-lib speech. Have in mind two or three major points that you want to get across in the finished story. Ask yourself, "If I could edit the article that will come out of this interview, what two or three sentences would I like to see?" Well in advance of the interview, write them out. Try to simplify and shorten them. Some people think if it is complicated it is clever. But Winston Churchill advised, "Short words are best and the old words when short are best of all."[9] Practice saying them out loud so they sound natural to the ear. Perfectly proper sentences in a written text are often too formal and cumbersome when spoken aloud. If it is a phone interview, keep them in front of you. Then at the earliest opportunity, try to capsulize your main points in answer to an interview question.

Place your most important points at the beginning of each response where they will be clear and isolated. In TV or radio interviews, this is especially important. Responses like "There are three reasons for that" invite poor editing. Rather say, "Price, performance, and reliability are the key factors in our decision."

Refer to the interviewer by name, early and often. In print this is a simple common courtesy. In TV it may help get that sentence past the editing process and onto the screen, since stations often like to show that their reporters are well known in the community. It also gives you some time to think before answering.

It is not only what you say but also how you say it that communicates. The effective speaker is not necessarily polished and perfect. He or she *is* energetic, involved and direct. Opera diva Beverly Sills, known as much for her candor as her charm, told *Time* magazine, "There is a growing strength in women, but it's in the forehead, not the forearm."[10] Says *New York Times* music critic Donal Henahan admiringly of Sills: "She never has any problem about what she means. She never fumbles for explanations."[11] A forthright, enthusiastic response to a question portrays candor and confidence—in your organization, in your position, in the reporter, in yourself. Long pauses before you answer or a stiff flat monotone indicate either a lack of conviction or a lack of interest. If the interview is being televised, this appearance of indecision and insincerity will be magnified.

You should not feel pressured to respond instantaneously to a difficult question on a complex subject. Although we have just mentioned the possible negative effect of a pause before answering, it is sometimes appropriate to take a moment to organize your thoughts. When you are making instant history—or instant policy—you have the right to be comfortable with the way you articulate your organization's role. In a print interview you can verbalize the pause by saying something like, "I hadn't thought of it from that viewpoint before...."

Think fast but talk slow. If the reporter is taking notes, it will help the accuracy. If you are being taped for broadcast—audio or video—it will help your audience's comprehension.

Never forget your ultimate audience. You are *talking* to a reporter, but you are *speaking* to the people who read the publication or watch the program—your past, present and potential customers, employees, shareowners and suppliers. (If none of these audience segments is being reached by the reporter's medium, you can legitimately ask your media relations person and yourself why you are doing the interview.) Frame your answers from *their* point of view, not your organization's. For example, say "Our *customers* now have three new colors to choose from," rather than "*We* have expanded our color selection." Or, "If this bill becomes law there will be significantly fewer parks where you can take your family," rather than "*Our industry* is opposing this legislation because ...".

Try to humanize your responses by giving a little bit of your own personality as well as the organization position. Your field is interesting to you. Make it equally interesting to the reporter. In addition to providing the reporter with a "quotable quote" you may help destroy the myth that all business people are stodgy and boring, particularly if you work for a large corporation. An excellent example occurred in 1982 when *New York Times* reporter Tom Friedman was interviewing AT&T executive Paul Zweier concerning the consent decree by AT&T and the Department of Justice that ended the antitrust suit. The price was divestiture of the Bell telephone companies, but the prize was no more restrictions on the company's entry into the data-processing business. Friedman asked Zweier what his initial response had been to the news. "My reaction to the restructuring was one word: 'Wow,'" Zweier responded. "We have been part of a patterned structure for a long time and somebody has just said: 'Here is an open door. If you guys want to, take this company somewhere else.' Now that's exciting."[12] Chrysler Corporation Chairman Lee A. Iacocca gave a similar notable and quotable response to NBC's Garrick Utley who asked, "What about mergers—any marriages yet?" "No," replied Iacocca, "but I think I've been kissed."[13]

Do not be embarrassed if a number or detail is not at hand. Simply tell the reporter that your media relations person will get it. Also, don't feel obliged to accept a figure or fact the reporter cites. Say you are not familiar with it and offer to have it checked also. Never—repeat, never—have other staff people in addition to the media relations person in the room with you. Surrounded by too many advisers, you may appear to be an obedient Gulliver surrounded by Lilliputians. The reporter wants *your* views and comments, not facts and figures, from the interview. Your delegating such follow-up detail means your train of thought will not be interrupted and you will be perceived as an expert not concerned with minutia. As well, it explicitly reminds the reporter that the media person is and should continue to be the one entrance point to the organization.

Do not let a reporter put words in your mouth. Whenever you hear the phrases, "Are you saying that . . . ?" or "Do you mean . . . ?" or "Isn't it really . . . ?" alarm bells should ring in your head. Mishandling this type of question can result in your feeling your words were reflected back by a fun-house mirror when the final story appears. If you do not like the way a question is stated, do not repeat it in your response—even to deny it. The reporter's question will not appear in print. Your answer will. It is better to respond in a positive way, using your own words, not the reporter's. For example, if a reporter asks if one of your products is overpriced compared to the competition, don't say "I wouldn't want to use the term 'overpriced.'" Instead, just say what you *would* want to say: "We believe our products provide high value for the price. For example [and go on to list the features]." This is particularly important in a television interview, when time constraints will force severe editing. You want to be sure your main point is right up front in every answer, in case you are on the air with only one sentence (it's called a sound bite in television jargon and an actuality in radio). Look back at this example to see what a one-sentence edit would do to you.

Look for the hidden agenda in questions. If a reporter is probing your recent hiring of salespeople proficient in certain skills, the resultant article may say that your company is in the midst of a marketing build-up to launch a new product line.

Keep your cool. A few interviewers—probably suffering from too much exposure to Mike Wallace's confrontation techniques on *"60 Minutes"*—deliberately frame their questions in emotional or accusatory tones. It is just a technique to get you to say something controversial. Do not let it work.

Avoid tongue-twisters. We have have all heard someone stumble on "specificity." And choose words with a minimum of "S"s so you do not sound like a hissing snake—an especially important hint for radio.

Avoid using jargon. When a reporter interrupts with what seem to be basic clarifying questions—or, in the case of an interview with a foreign reporter, if the interpreter pauses and looks puzzled—it may be that you have unconsciously dropped into obscure professional or industry jargon. To the neophyte, reading a wine list can be like interpreting a Russian code book (you know there are delicious secrets buried inside but you cannot get at them). Look for ways to explain your points with simple illustrations or analogies out of everyday life. As *Time* financial correspondent Frederick Ungeheuer put it: "Journalists are great simplifiers. We must take complicated technologies and explain them in a brief paragraph." In our highly technical business we have had success with comparisons such as, "The first transistors looked like little top hats on stilts" and "Today we can put all the intelligence of a room-size, hundred-thousand-dollar computer of the 1950s into a ten-dollar, cornflake-sized chip of silicon." Felix G. Rohatyn, the articulate investment banker from Lazard Frères & Company who helped lead New York City's perilous move from the edge of bankruptcy in the mid-1970s, even figured out how to describe that financial concept: "Bankruptcy is like someone stepping into a tepid bath and slashing his wrists—you might not feel yourself dying, but that's what would happen."[14]

Avoid negatives. "No, we are not discriminating against women" is not as convincing as "We have a broad program to actively recruit more women managers."

Consider what your words will mean to others. You don't want to be as parochial as Humpty Dumpty, who told Alice, "When I use a word it means just what I choose it to mean—neither more nor less." Frequently the same word can have different meanings to different audiences. A terminal in the computer business is a piece of equipment—but to many people it is a place where you catch a bus. William Safire offered another example: "To many a depression is what you take to a psychiatrist, not an economist."[15] And in the international arena there are classic stories of misunderstandings caused by a poor choice of words. If your organization actively sells its products or services overseas, you would do well to become familiar with the language, including local idioms, of your host countries.

Be realistic in your answers. Look at each question from the public's point of view. For example, if a reporter says "You don't have many black supervisors, do you?" don't counter with "Our record on that is terrific. We're doing much better than most companies." That sounds defensive. Instead, be positive in your answers. You might say "We still don't have enough black supervisors, although we are making progress. [Such and such] percent of our supervisors are black and we have these specific programs...."

Respond to a simple question with a simple answer. Short, simple answers are better than long, complicated ones. A few sentences using everyday language give the interviewer less opportunity to misunderstand you. And on TV, where time is measured in dollars, this is especially important. In fact, in a TV interview you should be sure to make your key points in less than a minute—preferably, in 20 or 30 seconds.

Never underestimate the intelligence of your audience—and never overestimate their knowledge. We are not suggesting you adjust your prose to the words used by high-school sophomores, but you must explain your terms, especially when you are covering a difficult subject. Two hours after a recent interview, a reporter phoned the media relations person to plead for a translation: "That interview reminded me of my college physics classes," she said. "I understood it while the professor was talking but when I got back to my room, I couldn't explain it."

Speak in the first-person, active voice. Avoid the passive, which places the doer of the action at the end of the sentence or sometimes eliminates responsibility altogether. Say *"We* will be moving our offices," not "Our *offices* will be moved." You want to portray your organization as a group of interesting concerned people who decide and do things, rather than a faceless, inanimate group. Similarly, don't duck responsibility for difficult actions. Say "*We* reluctantly have decided that a layoff of some of our employees is required," not "The *economy* has forced a layoff." Companies don't make decisions or establish policies—people do.

Do not waste your brief time with a reporter by arguing against the other side. You may want to refute their point of view but inadvertently end up giving valuable media exposure to their position. Instead, state your case positively, without mentioning your opponents at all. If you are forced to refer to your adversaries, avoid emotional labels such as "chauvinist" or "radical." Use "less experienced observers" or "the other side" instead.

Do not be offended by a reporter's questions about what you consider private or proprietary areas. As Robert MacNeil, of PBS's "MacNeil/Lehrer Report" explained in his autobiography, being a journalist is "a lifelong license to follow that most basic human trait, curiosity. . . . It is permission to probe and delve into whatever interests you as thoroughly or as superficially as you like . . . ."[16] True—but as a spokesperson it is your responsibility to decide how much you want to say in your answer. If the questioning moves into proprietary or confidential areas, simply explain that providing such information would be too helpful to your competitors. When the questioning gets too personal, wit can be a good defense. Ronald Reagan practices this technique with the best of them: "Our family didn't exactly come from the wrong side of the tracks," he said of his beginnings, "but we were certainly always within the sound of the train whistles."[17] Broadening your response to divert attention from the narrow, personal nature of the question is a good tactic—particularly during a television interview. A female politician asked how she balances her duties to her husband, children and the public might reply: "That question clearly illustrates the problems that so many American women who are working mothers face. . . ."

Do not respond to a narrow question with an equally narrow answer. Rather, take the opportunity to reiterate one of your key points. For example, if you are being interviewed on a plant closing and are asked how many people will be out of work, do not just say "about seven hundred." Instead, reply directly to the question and then immediately expand on it: "About seven hundred, but we are doing everything we can to help soften the blow. We will phase down operations gradually over the next six months.

And we are setting up an outplacement advisory group to help our people look for other jobs."

Do not answer hypothetical questions. Instead, particularize them with: "That's a hypothetical question so it is impossible to know what might happen. But let me tell you exactly what *did* happen in a similar case...."

Never, absolutely never, lie to a reporter. You may get away with it once or twice, but ultimately you will be found out. Then not only you, but also your organization, will have lost a priceless asset: credibility. As Winston Churchill put it: "To build may have to be the slow and laboring task of years. To destroy can be the thoughtless act of a single day."

Be yourself. If you like to sit around a conference table when you are meeting with your staff, that is likely a fine place for the interview; you will feel comfortable and the reporter will have a surface on which to write and/or place a tape recorder. If you prefer to emphasize your points by drawing diagrams on an easel, do it. If you love sports, it is perfectly appropriate to use an analogy from the football field to illustrate your point. If your taste leans more to music, feel free to make a comparison using an orchestra as a metaphor. The reporter wants *your* perspective—not that of a well-trained but impersonal robot who gives the impression of speaking fluently but formally in a foreign language.

HINTS FOR TELEVISION APPEARANCES

When you stare into the eye of a television camera and see that little red light go on, you are bluntly reminded that there is a huge audience out there which will see and hear whatever you say. In the early 1980s two-thirds of the American people relied on television as their primary source of news.[18] The "wiring of America" by cable companies, the concurrent increase in local programming, and the rapid expansion of electronic information services will combine to make television even more dominant in the American public's lives and thus, ever more important as an outlet for your organization's messages. Stage fright caused by the camera's relentless gaze and TV's wide exposure is natural, no matter how frequently you are videotaped, whether you are in the comfortable surroundings of your own office or the impersonal setting of a TV studio. But there are many things you can do in advance to prepare for the particular demands of television.

Appearances definitely *do* count on television. Consider, for example, the first Kennedy-Nixon debate in the U.S. presidential race of 1960. Polls showed that those who heard the debate on radio thought Nixon had won, whereas those who watched the event on TV named Kennedy the winner.

First of all is the choice of what to wear. Gone are the days when a man had to wear a light blue shirt. That requirement was caused by the fact that a bright white shirt would "burn in" a black and white camera—that is, keep it from getting a clear image because of a too-high contrast ratio. A blue shirt became *de rigueur* because in those days that was the only other color of shirt most male executives had. Now virtually all television programs are shot in color. Light blue is still a fine choice for both men and women. But most other colors are equally good. What you want to avoid are extremes—either small busy patterns or large, bold stripes on your tie, shirt, blouse or dress. Solid colors are best, but you should leave pure white or solid black home in the closet. Do not wear a large amount of jewelry, especially if it is bright, because it will cause the cameras to "flare," distracting viewers with a starburst of light. Women should wear dark-colored shoes; white or light colors tend to make your feet look large on screen. Men should wear calf-length socks in case you want to cross your legs on camera (remember the dictum that "leg shows are for women"). If you have a tan, do not get a haircut just before the interview in case your tan line is uncovered. Men with heavy beards should shave just before the crew arrives. Women should not wear too much make-up, especially eye shadow; the right amount for work is normally the right amount for television. Men should not refuse a little powder just before the cameras roll; if a TV technician makes the suggestion it means some perspiration is visible on the TV monitor's view of you—not surprising considering the bright lights and a normal amount of nervousness.

All of the techniques you practiced to help present your position persuasively to print journalists apply to television—only more so. Chicago civil rights leader Jesse Jackson knew that well: "If you had a camera with you I'd be talking differently," he told *Newsweek*'s Lea Donosky.[19] It is critically important that you make your points short and simple. TV's formula is to use perhaps 100 words from the reporter and a "sound bite" of 15 or 20 words from the speaker. Keep two facts in mind: First, television is a visual medium, so what the eye sees is as important as what the ear hears. And second, the camera magnifies whatever it sees. It sounds trite, but you should act naturally. Do not smile when it is not appropriate—you will look phony, not friendly. Do not gesture wildly nor move suddenly—the camera may lose you altogether. Do not stare upward into space when you are thinking—you will look like you are praying for divine guidance.

If you are being videotaped in your office, you or your media relations person should suggest other attractive areas of your operation for background footage. Television is at its best when it can show something happening. A picture of nothing but a person—a "talking head"—is visually boring. Your chances for coverage will be immeasurably improved if you make it easy for the program's producer to illustrate what you are saying. (That does not mean you should refer to complicated charts and graphs filled with detailed information, since it is unlikely they will be readable on the TV screen.)

Take a look at existing props in your office that may appear on camera if the interview is taped there. Family photographs add a warm touch. But a plaque with two small gold axes, once presented as an award for an expense-reduction program, can give the wrong impression if the interview is on layoffs or a plant closing.

Television is an intimate medium. You will be speaking not to the "general public" but rather to individual people—a family gathered together in the living room, a tired worker dozing in the den, someone catching up with ironing while watching the news. Eric Sevareid said he tried "to remember always that the public is only people, and people only persons, no two alike." Jim Scott, assignment editor of WISH-TV, CBS's affiliate in Indianapolis, offers this advice: "Talk one-on-one with the reporter. You are talking to an individual who is interested in what's going on, and thinks you have something of importance to say. Try to ignore the camera—or treat it as just somebody else who is looking on."

Normally the interview will be videotaped and then severely edited before being aired. Many times TV reporters will ask you the same question several times in different ways. They are giving their editors a variety of versions and lengths from which to choose. You should take the opportunity to sharpen your answer.

But no matter how often you are asked, you should always include your main point in each answer—right up front. It may be disconcerting to have the reporter pay more attention to a stopwatch than to your words and it may seem unnecessarily repetitive. But when the tape is edited, only one response will be left—and you and the reporter both want it to be a clear and concise statement.

Do not be intimidated by a reporter with a microphone during a fast-breaking "spot news" situation. An unnerving interview technique is to thrust the mike at you and then pull it back when the reporter has what he or she wants. You have two options in this situation: Gently take hold of the mike—over the reporter's hand if necessary—or smile and say "I haven't finished answering the last question yet," and go back to making your point.

Regardless of what reporters or TV technicians tell you, assume you are on the air all the time you are in their presence. An old ploy is to have the cameraperson tell you a small adjustment has to be made in the equipment: "It will only take a minute. I'll let you know when I'm ready, so just relax and bear with me." Then the reporter leans across and murmurs an "off the record" question with a smile. Remember, you are always *on* the record. Bright lights and a quiet room are no longer needed with the latest video hardware.

Sometimes attempts to be pleasant and polite can backfire. Try to avoid nodding as the reporter talks. It could be viewed on camera as acknowledgement of the premise behind the question. Similarly, be careful about saying "That's a good point" after a negative question. Tight editing could wipe out the rest of your response.

HINTS FOR RADIO

A radio interview has some different characteristics from either a phone interview with a print reporter or a televised taping. Unless it is a major news story, the station will use only a very brief segment (10 to 20 seconds) of your interview—although it is likely to rebroadcast the item several times. So it is even more important that you make your main points succinctly. Also, radio rarely uses the reporter's questions on the air. Before you answer you should pause a moment to be sure the questioner is through and you are not "stepping on that person's line." You will ensure cleaner edits and warm thoughts from the audio engineer.

You are not seen by anyone, so you can have your key points written out and handy where you can see them—but you must be careful not to rustle the pages because even soft sounds may be heard over the air. This is crucial if you are appearing on a call-in talk show, where the studio's powerful microphones can pick up and amplify even the tiniest noises, including the sound of swallowing when you take a drink of water. Practice out loud. If you sound awkward or must gasp for breath, shorten your sentences and eliminate difficult phrases. You want to guard against sounding like you are reading a prepared response—on the air you will sound terribly stilted. You should speak in a conversational tone as you would with a friend on the phone. During the interview you should gesture as you would during a normal conversation; it will help both your voice and your body to relax.

HINTS FOR NEWS CONFERENCES

When you are participating in a news conference, you have the obligation not only to answer reporters' questions but also to make a few opening remarks giving the purpose of the conference and formally announcing the news that caused it. Answering questions at a news conference is very similar to being interviewed except that you have more than one person asking questions and you are not in the comfortable surroundings of your own office. The opening remarks position of a conference is much like giving a brief speech. As you look out over the crowd of cameras, lights, microphones, and people peering up at you expectantly, you may feel like a robin perched on the edge of her nest looking into the hungry, gaping mouths of her babies. Much like the mother bird, your obligation is to feed the media—that is, provide them with news in an interesting way in the shortest period of time. The same techniques you use for interviews and TV appearances will serve you well here.

Several hours before the news conference, come to the room to familiarize yourself with the set-up. Work out signals with your media relations person as cues if you begin speaking too quickly or answering reporters' questions too abruptly. Then leave, and use the time to practice what you intend to say—and perhaps to go for a brisk walk to clear your mind.

Do not show up again until immediately before the news conference is scheduled to start. Don't mingle with reporters ahead of time. Whether you are introduced by your media relations person or open the news conference yourself is up to you. In any case, ignore the many microphones that are placed on the podium. Do not ask if everyone can hear you—it is the responsibility of the audio engineers and your media person to ensure all the mike levels are correct. Just begin your formal remarks, speaking slowly and clearly, and following your text fairly closely if it has been included in the press kit materials. Like any attentive participant, the TV camera will be focused on you. But if you become long-winded or the cameraperson's attention wanes, the camera will scan the listeners—particularly that station's reporter—for reaction shots. If things really get dull the little red light will go off as the technician turns the camera off altogether.

After your introductory talk, open the session up to questions. Use an open phrase like "Now I would be happy to try to answer your questions" or "What are your questions?" rather than the closed construction "Does anyone have any questions?" Ask the journalists to give their names and publications or stations as they are called on. Don't pace around or the microphones and TV cameras will have trouble following you.

If there are no questions right away, don't panic. The reporters probably are reviewing their notes on your opening remarks and framing questions that will appeal to their readers or viewers. Simply wait a few minutes (it will seem like hours) and then invite questions again. Or point to a reporter you know and say "Susan, you usually have a good question for me." If there still are none, thank the reporters for coming and say you are available for individual questions if they wish.

More likely, the questions will start popping several at a time. Once you select a reporter to ask a question, keep your eyes on him or her as much as possible while you answer. This will keep other reporters from interrupting and help the reporter's camera crew get both of you on tape if they so desire. Allow one follow-up question from that journalist—but then establish eye contact with another questioner so one person is not able to dominate. Use the reporter's name in your answer whenever possible. Do not be unnerved if someone moves around with a hand-held camera or even crawls up to the podium on hands and knees to adjust a microphone or test the lighting with a light meter. You probably will be asked several similar questions by TV people, because broadcast editors generally like to show their own reporters on the screen asking questions. So don't hesitate to repeat your key point in answer to each question—again, only one version will appear on each channel—and be sure *not* to say "As I said in response to an earlier question...."

If very few journalists have shown up, you should proceed as planned., But if the small turnout is obvious, you may wish to acknowledge it with a light comment such as "Ladies and gentlemen, it looks like you will have an exclusive by coming here today ..." and conduct the session in a less formal manner. Equally important is for your media relations person to be prepared with everything from extra chairs to press kits in case many more people than expected show up. But if they are nonmedia people, they should politely but firmly be kept out of the news conference room. Journalists do not appreciate an audience, which can create distractions and generate noises picked up by the sensitive TV and radio audio equipment. And you are likely to be nervous enough without having kibbitzers present.

Thirty minutes is the normal length of a news conference—although if questions are still coming you may decide to go a few minutes over the scheduled time. You can end the conference yourself or have your media relations person do so by announcing that you have time for one more question. In any case it is a good idea to mingle afterwards with reporters in case they want private interviews or individual on-camera shots of you talking with them. But remember that everything you say during these conversations is also on the record. Therefore, you should be no less careful with your comments than you were when you were at the podium.

PRIOR TO THE INTERVIEW

Media relations people should make it a routine practice to get together with the spokesperson for a briefing before the interview. Executives' calendars are crowded—but a half-hour meeting together before the reporter arrives is time well spent. It gives you both an opportunity to review expected questions, constructively critique proposed answers, look at alternative ways to highlight key points, and discuss the thrust of this particular journalist and article. You can also work out a plan to end the interview if the reporter appears to be getting long-winded or repetitive. You should remind the spokesperson to tell the reporter that follow-up information will come through you. For a phone interview you can alert the spokesperson not to be unnerved by a request to tape the conversation, or by the tap-tap of a typewriter or the plunk-plunk of a computer or word processor. Indeed, it is positive feedback that the reporter's questions are being well answered, since many journalists do not take notes until they hear a newsworthy comment.

If there will be photography, it also can be helpful to remind your spokesperson to be tolerant of what may appear to be strange requests to move objects or rearrange poses. The photographer is likely looking for ways to get an interesting picture out of what is essentially a routine setting. As *Fortune* magazine picture editor Alice George put it: "It takes a special talent to take an eye-opening picture of an assembly line or a boardroom. The only way I know how to deal with the problem is by hiring photographers who have a new way of seeing."[20]

DURING THE INTERVIEW

As was covered in Chapter 4, your role as media relations person during the interview is to make introductions and then let the reporter take over while you take notes, interjecting only if a statement needs clarifying, a number requires verifying, or a promise of follow-up information should be made. If you are physically near the spokesperson during a phone interview, you might want to pass a note if you believe the person has missed an opportunity to make a key point or made a statement that needs further explanation. A decision to tape the interview—whether or not the reporter is doing so—should be made with great care. Many reporters who consider a media relations person's taking notes a normal part of their business are offended if you ask to tape the session. But if you are reluctant to cooperate because a reporter or program has a reputation for distortion, you may want to insist on taping as a condition for your spokesperson to be interviewed.

FOLLOW-UP AFTER THE INTERVIEW

For the media relations person the job is not over after the interview; actually, it is only beginning from the point of view of your relationship with your spokesperson. At the same time you are following up on your obligations to the reporter, you should devote similar attention to the interviewee.

Right after the interview you should call your spokesperson with feedback—giving both your impressions (helpful for the next time) and the reporter's (whose reaction right after the interview is a good indication of the probable tone of the story and thus should be shared with the spokesperson). If the reporter was critical, you will want to think carefully about how much detail you pass along—and how. If the spokesperson is normally proficient but in this case was not, it may just have been a bad day and no value will come from rehashing errors. If you foresee a potential problem in the resultant coverage that you cannot resolve with the reporter, go ahead and mention it. Your spokesperson would rather be alerted in advance than blindsided when the story appears. If the spokesperson did a particularly bad job, either confusing the reporter with poorly stated points or blithely releasing proprietary information, you might do well to resolve to find a different spokesperson in the future for that area of your operation.

As soon as the story appears, check the quotes and facts for accuracy. If it is print coverage, always try to get a copy of the article to the interviewee in advance of wider circulation within your organization. Offer your reaction—and get the spokesperson's.

If it is radio or TV coverage, you can purchase a copy of the tape from the station as a courtesy for the interviewee or for your files. If you live in a large metropolitan area such as San Francisco, Los Angeles, Chicago or New York, you can purchase a transcript or a tape from companies which sell such services. If it is a print piece, buy copies of the newspaper or magazine yourself. Although you may not intend it, a request to the reporter for a copy of the article when it is printed implies that you do not think enough of the publication to purchase it. Some reporters on hard-to-get association or international publications, however, make it a practice to provide copies to a spokesperson featured in a major article.

INTERVIEW NO-NOS

Here are some topics to avoid when you are talking with reporters, since they inevitably cause misunderstandings.

- *Do not ask if you can review the story in advance. Just as the reporter cannot expect to see your annual report or latest product plans until you are ready to make them public, so you cannot have advance access to their reporting of the news.*

- *Do not mention how much your organization advertises in the reporter's medium. No reputable publication or station permits its editorial judgement to be influenced by advertising, and you may unwittingly insult the reporter's personal and professional codes of behavior.*

- *Do not tell broadcast reporters you think 30 or 60 seconds is too short a time to adequately tell your story. They are no more satisfied with the time constraints they work under than you are. Only 22 minutes of a half-hour network television news program is devoted to news; the rest is commercials. In a column for the Wall Street Journal, Dan Rather said that every night at every network good and important stories wind up on the floor because there's not enough time in the broadcast.[21]*

    Walter Cronkite, speaking in support of extending the evening news to an hour, said that "If we had more time, we could do a much better job. We'd make what we're broadcasting far more understandable and be able to give stories that need it greater depth."[22] But it is also true that businesses spend billions of dollars every year telling their stories and selling their products in 10-, 30-, and 60-second advertisements on TV and radio.

- *Do not tell a reporter you will provide written answers to questions if he or she will send them to you. The media is not in the business of taking dictation. And that type of exchange probably is too time-consuming to meet the news deadlines. In any case, it will make the reporters think you are hiding something because you will not talk face-to-face.*

- *Do not ask a reporter to keep what you say "off the record." Perhaps the public's perspective was permanently changed by so much talk of "deep background" in the Woodward/Bernstein chronicle, All the President's Men. Remember that the sole reason a reporter is interviewing you is literally for the record— that is, to write and produce a story for publication or airing that gives you and your organization's views on a particular subject. The shock waves resulting from the Janet Cooke/Pulitzer Prize episode with the Washington Post are likely to make editors even more adamant that their reporters identify their sources in all but the most unusual cases. Presidents and Secretaries of State may wish to continue demanding off-the-record status for their remarks, but it is a much safer practice for the rest of us to assume everything we utter will be attributed. Thus, we should not say anything we would not want publicly associated with ourselves or our organization unless we have a long relationship and a special understanding with a particular reporter.*

HOW TO AVOID INTERVIEWING TRICKS

The vast majority of all interviews are pleasant, nonthreatening experiences. But when the interview has not resulted in any news or interesting quotes, the reporter may reach down into his or her bag of tricks. When that starts to happen, you need to be prepared. Here are some techniques developed by Stephen C. Rafe and Walter J. Pfister, Jr., co-owners of the Executive Television Workshop, New York City.

Technique:	*Needling*
Example:	*"Oh, come now. Do you really expect us to buy that?"*
Response:	*Stick by your guns. Don't equivocate or vacillate. Say "Absolutely, [reporter's first name]," then go on to reinforce the positive point just made or make a new positive point.*

Technique: *False facts (unintentional or deliberate)*
Example: *"So your profits are seventy-two percent [Actually they were 11%, but up 72% from the comparable quarter last year.]*
Response: *Correct graciously and go to your positive point. Begin with "Perhaps I could clarify that for your viewers, [reporter's first name]," then go on to make a positive point about how the profits are used, about providing jobs, or about investing in research.*

Technique: *Reinterpretation of your responses*
Example: *"So what we have here is a possible epidemic."*
Response: *Avoid repeating loaded words. Say "[reporter's name], what we're saying is, six of our employees have developed a minor skin rash, which we discovered through our own in-plant medical program." And go on to make a positive point about caring for employees' well-being.*

Technique: *Putting words in your mouth.*
Example: *"So you're still dumping your garbage in the river then, aren't you?"*
Response: *Recognize that their effort is to get you to use words you would just as soon not say.*
               Don't argue. Instead, say: "Let's see what's at issue here, [reporters name], if I may," then make your positive point.

6

ETHICS

The Golden Rules of Media Relations

Des Traynor, deputy chairman of merchant bankers Guiness and Mahon, walked into the room accompanied by managing director Maurice O'Kelly. Traynor, undoubtedly one of Ireland's most interesting businessmen, had never given an interview to the press. Suddenly, he agreed without hesitation to this session so we settled back for an entertaining and informative couple of hours.

Pleasantries are exchanged as the coffee and biscuits arrive. The photographer arranges the bodies and the notebook is opened. The pen is poised to pick up every word, but Traynor calls a temporary halt to the proceedings.

"Just before we start," he says, "we'll lay down two ground rules." A voice in the back of our head tells us that something like this was bound to happen.

"This first rule is, we see the article before you print it." We then told Traynor that the second rule was, in that case, irrelevant.

It was nearly a great moment in journalism.

We never did that interview but we listened to Traynor's reasons for laying down conditions which he must have known would make the interview impossible. As far as he was concerned, the bank had done very well without the help of the press up to now. Giving an interview at this stage, he explained, could hardly benefit the company, but there was always the possibility that it

could have some adverse effect through our interpretation of some
of the information. In other words, there was nothing in it for
them.

Business and Finance[1]
Republic of Ireland
September 23, 1982

The problem with ethics is that they have to be considered a
problem. To have to embody ethics into one's code of behavior
suggests that ethics are separate from one's routine, day-to-day
standards. Ethics should be as normal and as unconscious as
shaking hands when first meeting someone.

Unfortunately, ethics are not that simple. What makes some
actions worthy of the thought process concerning ethical standards
are the degrees of importance attached to certain actions while
others are considered not of equal importance.

Chester Burger, Accredited Public Relations (APR), public
relations executive, suggests that "ethics are nothing but standards
of behavior, and who among us is qualified to suggest that his or
her standards deserve to be followed by others?"[2]

Dr. Albert Schweitzer offered his definition of ethics: "Ethics
is the name we give to our concern for good behavior." We feel an
obligation to consider not only our personal well-being, but also
that of others and of human society as a whole."

The Ethics Resource Center found that the general public
readily understands what ethics are. "More than eighty-six percent
of all people interviewed associated ethics with standards and rules
of conduct, morals, right and wrong, values and honesty. The
public also understood that if ethics appeared in the headlines the
story would tell about the *lack* of ethics—the doing of wrong as
opposed to right."

Ivan Hill, president of the Ethics Resource Center, believes
that "Honesty and ethics are basic, working social principles, not
just moral guidelines." He adds: "True, ethics involve more than
honesty but *without* honesty there are no ethics. When honesty is
left out of ethics, there is a smelly residue of hypocrisy. Such
hypocrisy creates a real danger in the efficient functioning and
manageability of an open society, especially in business and in
government."[3]

Examples of the lack of ethics abound. Most notable, and

perhaps the event with the longest reaching impact, was Watergate. Subsequent investigations have shown that throughout Watergate, the emphasis was on forcing the so-called solutions to fit the problem, rather than defining the problem and seeking a solution to it. It appears that at no point did anyone ask "Why are we doing this? Why are we putting layer upon layer of cover over this problem?"

Ironically, the newspaper which was so instrumental in the Watergate revelations, the *Washington Post*, found itself in the middle of an ethical dilemma when a reporter, Janet Cooke, created and was able to have printed a totally fictitious tale of an eight-year-old heroin addict—an article which won for her the Pulitzer Prize for feature writing.

The difference between these two events is in how they were handled when the problem was discovered. For, after Cooke admitted the story was fiction, the Pulitzer Prize was returned, the newspaper took its share of the responsibility, and the journalist and the newspaper agreed to part ways. Whereas both President Nixon and Cooke share ignominy as people who have practiced unethical behavior, the newspaper emerged as showing and practicing a high regard for ethical behavior.

It appears that one way to create a standard of ethical behavior is to learn to not practice behavior considered by the majority of people to be *un*ethical. Because what constitutes ethical behavior and what does not is debatable, we will attempt only to suggest certain guidelines for preferred behavior when dealing with the media. Even these guidelines will be argued by some, depending on experiences, country of origin, individual philosophies, and so forth. However, we have found from our own experience that these guidelines work the best for us.

TRUST EACH OTHER

There is a story told of animal trainer, Clyde Beatty, who was asked by a reporter: "Mr. Beatty, even though you deal with lions and tigers as though they were kittens, surely you're afraid of something—spiders or snakes or something. What are you afraid of?"

Beatty replied: "Son, I'm afraid of those lions and tigers."[4]

Fear and respect are often synonymous. His respect for the

power and intelligence of big cats helped Beatty to work with them, not against them.

The same is true with the media. The media are poweful and because they are powerful they must be respected. But to fear the media is to put yourself in the position of the down-trodden or the subservient. Your true position is that of a professional exchanging information with another professional.

Trust the representatives of the media. They are performing a job, not staging a lynching.

LYING

Because an adversarial role exists between many organizations and the media, people often think the way to attack the adversary is to lie to him or her. A rationale for such convoluted thinking escapes us, but it does exist.

A lie is a lie is a lie. No good comes of lying; particularly, no good comes from lying to the media. A lie will come out in print or on television. It will be taken as truth by the public who, when they later discover the real story, will disbelieve anything further that the organization says.

Joseph Sullivan, writing in *Business and the Media*, reminds us: "First, businessmen must realize that both reporters and the public are sophisticated enough to recognize smokescreens, if not penetrate them. Honesty *is* the best policy."[5]

A public relations executive from Chicago adds: "What we do know is that honesty and candor between the media and business form a bond that tends to grow stronger with good experience."[6]

Lying in public is no different from lying in the courtroom under oath. The sentence, however, can be tougher: loss of credibility, loss of respect, loss of customers, loss of trust by the community, and by shareowners. There is no such thing as a "half-lie," a "small lie" or a "white lie." The adjective does not detract from the noun, rather, the adjective enhances it.

Watergate produced one of the better examples of the attempt at a half-lie: the use of "not at this point in time." This qualifier specifically defines the scope of the statement given, thus producing a built-in defense of the statement later. For example:

"Are you negotiating to buy out XYZ Company?"

"We are not contemplating buying out XYZ Company at this point in time."

This response begs the question: Will you contemplate a buy-out later? Have you already considered the question? Have you actually bought out the company and are denying only contemplating a buy-out?

There are other ways of handling this situation, such as giving a stand-by statement that you are holding talks with the XYZ Company. Such a statement will satisfy the reporter's needs and prevent you from backing yourself into a half-lie corner.

TO COMMENT OR NOT TO COMMENT

Few words create such frustration to a reporter as "No comment." A reporter is trying to do his or her job. A key element in that process is for the reporter to ask questions and for the respondent to answer those questions. For a reporter to hear "No comment" is the same as giving a welder a job to do and then refusing to allow that welder to have access to the pieces that need welding.

The problem seems to rest in the connotation the phrase "No comment" has. It is assumed by many people to be a safeguard against putting one's foot in one's mouth. For instance, saying "No comment," seems safer than saying "I don't know what you are talking about," or "I made a mistake," or "The company regrets that it made a decision fifty years ago which has adverse effects today," or "We prefer to not discuss that topic."

Reporters and the general public have assumed, because of the misuse of the phrase, that "No comment" really means "I am guilty as hell but I won't admit it."

The simpler course to take is to answer the reporter's questions. If you do not know the answer, reply "I don't know." The more information you can provide, however, the less the reporter can speculate about your activities. Following is a list of sample situations with examples of ways to avoid "No comment":

1. *Rumors of an imminent layoff or plant shutdown.* "When we have any such announcement, I will let you know at once. I am sure you understand that our procedure is to

let the employees know first so they don't hear the news on radio or television."

2. *Employee arrest for stealing, drugs, etc. on or affecting your organization's property.* Confirm facts like date, time, and number involved in the arrest that would be readily available to a reporter at the police stations, as well as the employment status of your people. Then: "We are cooperating fully with the appropriate agencies [name them] in the investigation. Beyond that, it would be best for you to talk with the local police [or whomever] for further information."

3. *Employee activity (positive or negative) not affecting your organization.* Confirm employment and job title only. Then: "We do not give out any additional information about our employees, because we feel doing so might intrude on their privacy."

4. *Sales results, production plans, and other proprietary information.* "I hope you can understand but to tell you that would give our competitors too much valuable information about our sales plans" [or manufacturing processes, or marketing strategies, or whatever].

5. *Information from an employee.* "That's an individual's opinion. The company believes . . ."

6. *Rumors of imminent dividend action, stock offering, debt issue, merger, etc.* "We have nothing to announce at this time. You are well aware that there are clear procedures [prior notification of the stock exchange on which a company's shares are traded, simultaneous release to the financial and business wire services, etc.] for any announcement that could affect our stock price or an investment decision."

7. *Frivolous charges.* Respond with "That's absurd," or "That statement is so ridiculous that I won't dignify it with a response," or even "That's hogwash!"

8. *Inappropriate questions.* "Our organization has no position on that issue one way or the other" is an appropriate answer to questions about political, social, religious or other issues on which a public position might unnecessarily alienate segments of the public. Also, "We are in the business of telecommunications [or whatever],

not religion." Or, "We are apolitical in our marketing."

9. *Leaks of settlement plans or other bargaining
   information.* "We are negotiating with the union in good
   faith to resolve the issues that separate us. Certainly we
   all want to avoid a strike. I shall confine any other remarks
   to the bargaining table where I hope they will contribute
   to the negotiation process."

10. *Advance publicity prior to a new product announcement.*
    "The company has made no such announcement." Or,
    "We have read those reports with great interest." Or, "You
    know you are always among the first to know whenever
    we are ready to go public with new product plans."

11. *Question on a judicial or regulatory ruling.* "We will have
    to study the decision [or ruling, or judgment] before we
    can discuss it in detail."

WHEN YOU HAVE TO SAY NO

As a media relations spokesperson, do not confuse "No comment"
with "No, I can't answer that question because . . ." There are
legitimate times when information cannot be disclosed; reporters
know and respect those times.

In an effort to make sure cases are tried in the courtroom and
not in the media, many judges now are imposing restrictions on the
parties in the action which prevent any discussion of the case with
the media. Either party found guilty of ignoring this restriction
often can be charged with contempt of court. Thus, if a reporter
asks about a court case, it is perfectly understandable and permiss-
able to reply: "I'm sorry but we're not allowed to discuss this case
under terms agreed to in the court." You are not commenting on
the subject, nor are you stone-walling; rather, you are explaining to
the journalist why, in this instance, you cannot be of help.

Similarly, if you are asked about talks between your company
and another, you can respond: "I'm sorry, but we have agreed to
keep our business discussions private." This often will be the case
as companies considering major agreements, alliances, or acquisitions declare at the outset that no material will be issued to the
media unless jointly agreed to by the parties.

Another instance of being able to say no without guilt is when the information sought is specifically proprietary. For example, if your company has been purchasing large quantities of aluminum for its products for more than a decade and then suddenly decreases its purchases of aluminum while increasing its supply of a less costly material, then the competition could assume one of many things: that your company is offering a new product line, that it has found a less expensive way to produce the same product, or is having some difficulty as yet to be determined. Whatever the answer, it is the type of thing you would not want to have in the press because it is damaging to your company's welfare.

Some cases of employee privacy also allow the spokesperson to say no to a reporter's request. More and more, employees are seeking to disassociate themselves with their jobs. This separation of person and job can cause some gnashing of the teeth when it comes to answering a journalist's legitimate inquiry and simultaneously respecting the employee's right to privacy.

A well-known, but not as well-used, procedure to protect all parties concerned during a photography session is the model release. This paper, when signed by an employee, allows the company to use the employee's photograph in advertising, training, or general publicity or for any other causes stated in the release.

Such a release is not sought for written material, however, and perhaps it should be.

Questions about a job function can be answered without concern for any one person who happens to hold the job. Questions about the job function as it relates to the person performing the job should be handled differently. For example:

"What is this particular piece of equipment?"

"It's a word processing unit for our central communications room."

"How have your employees responded to this equipment?"

"Not well. The equipment seems to be too tough for them and we've had to put them through training many times."

"May I talk to one of the employees?"

This is an obvious dilemma. Already you have given the impression that your employees are not capable of being trained on the equipment. To gladly agree to an interview on behalf of the employees would be disastrous. Ask the employees first, explaining carefully what the interview will be about so *they* can decide if they want to appear in public.

Obviously, a media spokesperson does not reply to any employee question which is beyond the realm of the spokesperson's responsibility. For instance, a question about an employee's financial status or personal habits must be referred to that employee.

MAKING DEMANDS

The example at the beginning of this chapter of a gentleman who wished to place restrictions on the interview is more common an occurence than one might suspect.

In many organizations, some upper-level or executive management person reviews the material which is written for internal use, such as the employee newspaper, management newsletter, benefit pieces, or internal magazine pieces. The annual report, an external vehicle, is also closely scrutinized by top management before being allowed to be sent to the world. It is easy to understand then, how executives might assume they have a right to review a reporter's copy. Sadly, this natural desire to make sure the material is accurate, fair, and legally defensible, often creates a totally different impression on a reporter.

Clearly, it is the responsibility of the media relations spokesperson to educate the management about the differences between a reporter and an in-company staff writer, the different audiences being served by each, and the rules under which each operates.

Andy Rooney, of "60 Minutes" fame, was once asked if he thought the manner in which the management of a large corporation dealt with him in imposing limitations on the questions to be asked, damaged that company in any way. Rooney replied: "It made me suspect they had something to hide. To this extent it damaged them. And because it was difficult to get information from them, I got it from a dozen less sympathetic sources . . . former executives of the company, drivers, pilots, and dissidents from within the company itself."[7]

Instead of making demands about an interview, you should make *clear* the subject matter of the interview, the time allowed for it, and what the material will be used for. This is good common sense in establishing interviews and both you and the reporter will be glad for the understanding. Also, while you should not ask to see a story before publication, you can suggest to the reporter that you are available to check quotes, facts, and figures at the reporter's convenience.

You can also remind your management that the only way to see copy in advance and assure that it says exactly what you want it to, is to buy advertising space and create the ad.

OFF THE RECORD

We practice the theory that there is no such thing as "off the record."

There is still controversy concerning the use of "off the record," evidenced by the definition of the term given to foreign journalists by the U.S. Foreign Press Center:

> The flat rule is that the material is *not for publication,* it is solely for the reporter's private knowledge. The off the record interview or briefing is most commonly used by officials to advise reporters of something that is going to happen so that they have the background or information necessary for planning purposes to cover the event when it does occur. For example, an official may explain that the Secretary of State is going to the Far East on a given date and that he will be talking about specific topics. The reporter cannot print that news since it is off the record, but he or she can make plans to follow along on the same trip and to report on the speeches and press conferences that the Secretary of State may hold.[8]

Obviously, there are times when you must give background material to a reporter before he or she fully understands a subject. That material should be as free from concern as what you are saying today. The same rules apply for background material as they do for current material: you do not give out proprietary information, legally restricted material, or material which would jeopardize an employee's privacy. Everything left over, then, should be available for publication. In short, everything left over should be *on* the record.

If you are in doubt about which way to go, then use this

guideline: Never say anything to a reporter you are not willing to see in print or hear on the evening news. This guideline should apply at all times, even in social settings, for reporters are creatures of habit and are seeking information from any available source. They are doing their job 24 hours a day as should you.

Another argument about "off the record" contends that using this ploy will curry favors with reporters. We disagree on several counts:

1. Being an effective media relations spokesperson depends on building trust and credibility, not building a "favors" list.
2. Telling a journalist information "off the record" cannot help but imply that there is still *more* information not yet released or perhaps even being told to another reporter.
3. Not all journalists will honor an "off the record" request. Many people know, from bitter experience, what the results of this can be.

ADVERTISING

The temptation to use the media for free advertising is a great one. Resist it mightily. The media are there to report news, not release your organization from a financial obligation to advertise. If your announcement does not qualify as newsworthy, do not send it out; instead, buy advertising space. For example, if a store is closing for two days to inventory, it should make that announcement to its customers through advertising. Such a closing is not news because it is not unique, not different, not unusual.

Conversely, do not try to use your advertising might to blackmail the media into thinking your way. It will not work. A disagreement with the media about how a story on your organization was handled should not come down to a "Well, if you don't change that story, we'll pull all our advertising." Such a threat hurts only your organization as you lose a prime way to reach your customers at a time when you possibly need them (you would not be threatening such a move if the story was favorable, would you?).

Along those same lines, do not assume that because your organization advertises with a certain medium that your releases will always be run with that medium. A news release must be determined on its own merits, not on its association with another department.

THE GOLDEN RULE

At this point, you should be realizing that most of what has been discussed really comes down to this: Do unto others as you would have them do unto you.

Just as you seek help in performing your job, so does a reporter. The reporter looks to you for assistance and giving that assistance is your job. Make the situation easier for both of you by remembering that you are not dealing with an enemy, someone you have to defeat. You are dealing with another human, one who wants to be treated with the same courtesy and respect as you would like to be shown.

7 SPECIAL EVENTS

How to Make Them Work for You

At a gala event at Radio City Music Hall in New York City, Coca-Cola Co. announces it will market a product called Diet Coke. CBS and AT&T unveil a home information system that allows consumers to check restaurant prices, shop at department stores, pay bills, and access the latest news using a simple terminal in their homes. Sony introduces a new portable video camera that lets amateur photographers shoot moving pictures with sound and then instantly show the results on their television sets. For each of these events, reporters are invited to "taste and touch" to celebrate the occasion—with the expectation that they will go back to their publications or stations and write news stories that will spread the word to the general public.

Your organization may not have such dramatic new products to show off, but you too can hold a special event to generate positive media coverage. In addition to new product announcements, a plant opening, new CEO, dignitary visit, open house or planned expansion all are fine reasons to host a celebration and news conference. These special events are staged occurrences, so you usually control the timing. They are held to promote good news, so you are on the offensive, not the defensive. They tend to have a more casual, party-type atmosphere to encourage person-to-person dialogue between the news media and your organization's executives. Working on special events is fun. The trick is to also make it profitable for your organization in terms of positive news media coverage, improved public opinion or increased sales.

There are two keys to getting the most effective media relations results from special events. First, clearly enunciate your information objective and then evaluate every idea by whether or not it helps meet that objective; and second, keep running lists that track progress and responsibility for all planned and possible activities. You must constantly think in generalities while at the same time living in detail. Michelangelo is said to have counseled a young artist: "Perfection is made up of details." It will be your ability to keep sight of the forest and every single tree that will make the event a success from a media viewpoint—and well worth the expense from your organization's perspective.

If your company's stock is traded publicly, you may also want to coordinate with those colleagues responsible for relations with the financial community. Reporters frequently call security analysts and market experts for an outside objective evaluation—and quotable quote—to include in their story on a major corporate announcement. Thus it is to your advantage to keep financial analysts who follow your company and industry fully informed about your news, preferably on announcement day. You can either have copies of the press kit delivered to key financial analysts or arrange a separate restaging of the news conference for them. (It is normally not wise to invite journalists and security analysts to the same announcement event. Their interests are different and they deserve individual attention.)

ANNOUNCING A NEW FACILITY

Announcing the purchase of property and the building of a new facility provides unparalleled opportunities for positive media and community relations. It also serves as a fine example of how to plan a special event. In particular, it will tax your abilities if you find yourself operating in new territory without the benefit of established relationships with local reporters and editors (or even knowledge of the local geography) if the move is an expansion into a state or country in which your organization has not operated.

Integral to your planning should be the knowledge that your plans are very likely not going to be kept a secret until your announcement day. If the deal is a big one—in terms of size of the property, prestige of the company or number of potential jobs, for example—you should count on the fact that there will be a leak. Real estate agents showing property, local boards approached for zoning regulations, a hotel visited to evaluate conference facilities, a pilot hired for aerial photographs of the site—all these provide ample opportunities for the news to slip out no matter what precautions your organization takes. You should have approved and ready for immediate use a stand-by statement in case a reporter calls seeking your comment on rumors. If your plans are so uncertain that you do not even have an announcement date tentatively set, you should probably say nothing more than that your organization is looking at a number of potential sites for possible future expansion, but no plans are firm yet. If you have a timetable in mind, you might want to go further by adding that you will let the reporter know when a decision is made and an announcement is imminent.

You also will want to develop a solid relationship early on with others involved in the project. People from such disciplines as real estate, legal and finance, either on your organization's staff or retained for this job, will become critical resources as announcement time draws near. Your involvement in the planning stages helps build their confidence in you and your contribution to the project's successful conclusion. It also makes it more likely you can get their early concurrence on an objective and working strategy—not to mention their personal involvement in the implementation of your information plan.

Once you know the announcement is a "go"—even before you have a firm date—you should immediately develop a check list of all activities which need to be undertaken, and write down any related issues that must be considered. This will be your overall master list. It will spawn a number of more detailed "to-do" lists for many of the entries. Included on your master list should be the following:

1. *Date/time of announcement.* Probability of bad weather? Other conflicting events such as a holiday or an election?

Best time for the local news media? Availability of key participants?

2. *Site of announcement*. Your organization's headquarters or at location of new property? On-site or in a hotel or commercial establishment? Ease of accessibility for guests and news media? Fire or other emergency exit procedures? Facilities for the handicapped?

3. *Main theme*. Expansion of your organization into new territory? New business? Move from older facility?

4. *Guests*. Federal, state and local government officials? Key community and business leaders? Local people helpful in site selection? News media—local? national? trade? Other VIPs? Employees? Spouses? Financial and security analysts?

5. *Speakers*. Only your organization's executives? Governor or top state or federal official? Mayor or local official?

6. *Type of occasion*. News conference alone? With lunch or dinner? Reception? Local customs on food and alcohol? Budget restrictions?

7. *Media relations*. Press kit materials? Sound and lighting facilities for electronic media? Transportation to site?

8. *Invitations*. Written or by phone? Special arrangements with typing pool? RSVPs required? Separate for news media? For head table?

9. *Mementos*. Appropriate? Cost? Different ones for media or VIPs? In keeping with theme? Time to engrave or personalize? Place on tables if meal, or distribute as guests leave?

10. *Arrangements if travel involved*. Hotel and travel reservations for your organization's executives? Fruit basket or similar welcome gift in rooms? Other VIPs? Spouses? The media? Pre-registration courtesies? Billing arrangements? Late checkouts?

11. *Collateral materials*. Exhibit? Printed program? "Who we are, what we do" brochure on your organization for guests? Place cards at table settings? Name tags? Reserved table signs? "Working press only" sign outside news conference room?

It is a good idea to ask others who will be involved to review your list to see if you have left anything out or overlooked any local customs. Next you should establish an information objective and budget, assign responsibility for each of the activities, develop an overall timetable and set specific due dates. Then you must oversee implementation on virtually a day-to-day basis to ensure everything gets done on time.

Guidelines to Follow

1. Make sure the objective for your information effort is supportive of your organization's goals and your overall media relations plan, and is agreed to by everyone involved. It should include both your key message and target audience. Before making any decision, evaluate it against that objective. For example, when we were discussing possible speakers for the official opening of AT&T's Network Software Center in Illinois in 1982, someone suggested we invite the vice president of the United States "to get publicity" since it was an election year. Our goal was not, however, publicity for the sake of publicity. If it were, we pointed out, we could do something bizarre like have an employee run across the speakers' platform in the middle of the ceremony. Rather, our objective was to get media coverage on our emerging software expertise and the contributions it will make to new Information Age communications services for the public. Having the vice president speak—*particularly* because the ceremony would take place only a few months before a federal election—could divert attention from our software message and focus it on politics. Thus, it might inhibit rather than support our information objectives. Better to invite the president of Bell Laboratories to join our CEO on stage so the speakers would personify the high-technology partnership that will deliver AT&T's products to the marketplace.

2. It is usually good politics as well as good media relations to invite the governor of the state, or the mayor or chief county official, to make a few brief remarks. It is wise to try to restrict a politician to a 5-minute official welcome rather than the keynote address; this way you control the length of the program and the main message the media takes away from the event.

3. Choose your speakers and spokespersons very carefully. Then provide them with solid background information and help them practice (see Chapter 5).

4. Do not let yourself be distracted by clerical tasks that can be delegated to others, such as travel arrangements or hotel reservations for VIPs. Conversely, you will want to maintain oversight to the extent that you are comfortable all these details are taken care of.

5. Supervise all aspects of the news conference personally, from the opening statement to the contents of the press kit. Anything affecting the information effort is your business, regardless of who is responsible. You may be the only person with the complete picture.

6. If a tour is part of your program, time it with a group the size of those who will move around together on the big day rather than by walking the planned path alone. Keeping a group of people together (and rounding up stragglers) can be time-consuming and throw you off schedule.

7. Severely limit the number of officials introduced individually or allowed to speak as part of the news conference or ceremony. Such so-called obligatory recognition is terribly boring to the audience—and normally not required at all. Better to have your emcee or the organization's top speaker use one general statement to thank "all the local people who made us feel so welcome" or commend "the employees whose dedication and talent made this event possible." To have public officials or key executives feel they are getting VIP treatment, you can reserve a special table for them at the luncheon or have your CEO thank them personally after the ceremony.

8. Arrange early on to document with still photography (black-and-white and color) and film or videotape each stage of a new facility, from architect's drawings to model to groundbreaking through construction and official opening. Such a photographic history will be invaluable not only to meet the needs of the news media but also for your annual report or other external and internal information materials.

9. If there will be a meal after the news conference, put "Reserved for press" cards on tables nearest the podium or head table. Do not assume reporters will stay for the meal just because they are coming to the news conference. Ask them to RSVP to the news conference and luncheon or reception separately.

10. If you are having a meal, review the schedule with the catering person in extreme detail. Specify serving times and forbid

any clearing off of tables while the speeches are underway. Many a first-class occasion—and potential television or radio coverage—has been ruined by the sound of clattering dishes.

11. Review and update your check lists often. The ball takes some funny bounces on occasion, and the only way to track it is to always keep it in sight. Conduct frequent meetings where everyone involved shares progress reports. If your committee is physically separated, issue written status reports and have telephone conference calls. Occasionally send written progress reports to your organization's top executives.

12. If it is possible, arrange for a separate room for individual private interviews between your CEO and selected reporters after the news conference. Allow time in your schedule for such interviews between the news conference and the meal, perhaps by scheduling a reception between the two.

13. Try to have a separate "working room" for storage of press kits, mementos and other office materials such as a typewriter and blank news release paper in case you have to revise the release at the last minute. If your event is taking place at a commercial establishment, get permission from the manager to ship ahead as much of your material as possible.

14. Have plenty of copies of your business card—which should carry your home telephone number—to give to the media. Try to get time to chat with any reporters you have not met before. The relationships you begin to develop at the announcement ceremony will serve your organization well as construction proceeds—especially if you face unfortunate events like an accident or a union problem, or will be communicating mostly by telephone if your office is not near the new facility.

15. Understand that the primary focus of reporters' questions will be on the economic advantages of your news to the community in terms of jobs, taxes and related support services. Anticipate their needs by being prepared to give our general figures and a probable timetable. But do not lock yourself into a potential problem of appearing to renege on a promise a few years hence by being overly specific at announcement time. Use round numbers: "We expect to hire about a thousand people over the next two years" is better than, "We plan to hire 1083 people by yearend 1988," unless you are positive your figures will not change. Also, for local taxation purposes be careful about placing a value on your

project until your design and construction plans are firm and you have consulted with a tax expert.

16. Keep track of your expenditures and get approval before making commitments over your budget.

17. If you decide to give a memento to the media or to guests, personalize it so that recipients are reminded of your organization when they use it. Pens or pocket calculators carrying your logo are useful, and they can be inserted into the press kit if you want to give them only to reporters. Tote bags are especially good giveaways because they are carried and the message can be seen. At the announcement of a new electronic components plant in Florida, we gave guests a pewter plate engraved with, "Western Electric and Orlando—Partners in new telecommunications technology." That theme was picked up in the news conference announcement, luncheon keynote address, lobby exhibit, on the press kit folder and in the program. To take advantage of the new product's name, at AT&T's introduction of the Merlin communications system we gave reporters heat-sensitive mugs on which a message "magically" appeared when coffee was poured in.

18. Arrange for photography—still and video or film—of the news conference and announcement ceremony.

19. Make sure the head table and news conference setup photographs well so that you get maximum exposure for your organization's message. The lectern should carry your logo, not the hotel's. If the drapes behind the announcement area have a busy pattern or inappropriate color, put up portable curtains or an attractive sign with your theme or organization's name behind the speakers. All visuals should be simple, with copies included in the press kit. View the staging through a camera's eye—literally if necessary.

20. Provide three or four phones for the media's use. Arrange for at least one line for the exclusive use of your organization's executives, the governor or other top government officials and their key aides.

21. Have a reception table where at least one person stays to direct guests to coatrooms and bathrooms, control access to private phones, take messages, and provide other logistics support. Give this person photos of VIPs who should get special care if the receptionist does not know them.

22. Set up a separate table with another dedicated person

who will help you handle press kit distribution, requests for private interviews, or any other courtesies that should be extended to working journalists.

23. You can have a first-class press kit folder and also save money by carrying a photograph or drawing of the new facility along with your organization name on the cover—but *not* including the date of the event. That way you can arrange for production of the kits before a final date is set to avoid rush-job printing charges and keep your last-minute duties to a minimum. You also can use the folders for other occasions such as open houses or background information packages for the media as construction proceeds or new reporters request materials.

24. Just before the event, write out a final detailed chronology of every activity related to announcement day. Include arrival and departure times of your organization executives and other VIPs, limousine arrangements, and the agenda timed to the minute. Give copies to everyone involved—including limo drivers, the hotel catering manager, and the person at the guest reception table.

25. Prepare a separate package of materials for your key executives involved in the program. Include the press kit and detailed agenda—and also private background and Qs and As that could come up, key officials and reporters deserving personal attention (with nicknames and phonetic spelling if their names are difficult to pronounce), potential local concerns such as environmental issues or union problems, and their individualized itinerary and schedule—with a reminder of the times they should be available for separate media interviews. Give a copy of this package to the executive's secretary or chief staff person, along with the private phone number reserved for their use—and keep a few extra copies with you in case they are misplaced.

26. Coordinate the agenda and schedule closely with the press secretary or chief aide of government officials who are participating in the program. Inquire about security or other special arrangements you should make. For example, governors or top federal officials often are accompanied by security as well as staff wherever they go, so they need to be included in your meal count.

27. Well in advance circulate a proposed invitation list to key people who can provide counsel on who should be included. In

some communities, for example, the sheriff or chairman of a local regulatory agency can be as influential as the mayor or county commissioner. Divide the list into categories: business and civic leaders; federal, state and local government officials; people directly involved in site selection or facility design such as industrial development commissioners, architects and real estate people; community leaders such as educators and clergy; working press who will be invited separately to the news conference (as compared to publishers and station owners, who normally are included in the civic or business leaders category).

28. Arrange for set-up time and personally inspect all the facilities the night before and day of the event. Test the sound and lighting arrangements for TV and radio. If your CEO is flying in, consider meeting the plane and taking advantage of the drive time to the announcement site for a last-minute briefing. Read the local papers and alert your CEO to any noteworthy current issues.

29. Arrange for separate distribution of the press kit to reporters not attending the event at the time of or just after your news conference. Only in rare cases should you allow advance distribution, or you will hurt chances of the media's covering the event in person.

30. Monitor that evening's television news programs. Arrange for video tapes of TV shows and audio tapes of radio coverage. Get copies of the daily papers. Within 24 or 48 hours provide your organization's top executives with samples of initial news coverage of the event—plus a video tape of the full news conference and ceremony if you made one. Consider a separate, shorter version for showings to your employees or the board.

31. Promptly after the event write thank-you letters for your organization's CEO's signature to key dignitaries who participated in the program, and to those who worked with you to make the occasion a success.

32. A month or so after the event, when all the press clippings have been gathered, put together a summary for your organization's officers and board that includes information objectives and a brief analysis of how they were met, with selected samples of news media coverage.

33. Announcements of a new facility are significant occurences in any organization, so consider putting together a formal scrapbook to commemorate the event. After circulation to

your executives and board, it could be given to the new plant manager or included in your organization's official archives.

34. Set up a system to handle the inevitable queries from real estate agents, relocation people, job applicants, banks, and other prospective product and service suppliers that will be generated by the news coverage of your announcement.

35. Put together a complete file including everything connected with the occasion, from your private memos and check lists to the press kits and the official announcement speech. It will be invaluable not only as a record of an historic event but also as a model for planning future announcements.

SPECIAL EVENTS SUCCESS STORIES

Far too often publicity efforts surrounding modernization or expansion programs are mostly cosmetic. News coverage and public interest is generated by one big event, but once the decorations have been put away from the last open house everyone goes back to business as usual. In effect, the whole exercise has been "more show than go." Such was not the case, however, with the public relations program at Herrick Memorial Hospital in Berkeley, California. It had the traditional image-improvement objectives of many PR plans, but it was grounded in solid research. It involved the introduction of ongoing preventive health care information programs. And it was backed by a change in the hospital's name that symbolized an enhanced mission to educate the healthy as well as treat the sick.

The hospital had been a significant force in the San Francisco East Bay Area for the better part of a century. Founded by a man whose interest in medicine had been prompted by the death of his wife, the facility opened in 1904 in an ornate Victorian mansion under the name of Roosevelt Hospital. Later it was renamed Herrick Memorial in honor of its founder.

The construction of a new $14-million, 153-bed wing in the spring of 1980 offered a perfect opportunity to update its image and bring its many publics—including the news media—to the hospital to see the new orientation of the staff and facilities. "A community survey and staff interviews showed that Herrick had an unclear or nonexistent reputation with many of its publics," explained Gloria

Dunn, then director of community and public relations for the hospital. "The issue was viability. We had to become better known so we could increase usage of our services." Thus the effort met the ultimate test of a good public relations program—it directly supported the organization's overall purpose and profitability.

Dunn developed a broad plan which she presented to the hospital's administration, board of trustees, and medical executive board for approval. Heading the list of action items was a recommendation to change the name of the hospital from Herrick Memorial to Herrick Hospital and Health Center. "We needed to remove the death connotation inherent in the word, 'memorial' and add the positive philosophy implied by 'health center,'" Dunn said. She sold the decision makers on the name change because it provided advantages for the institution to (*a*) derive image advantages from a name that conveys a clear statement of purpose; (*b*) demonstrate the hospital's expansion and change of direction; and (*c*) offer to those involved with the hospital a reason for association—pride for employees, physicians, trustees, and patients; and encouragement to donors and volunteers. The plan also included a new logo with the Herrick "H" extending an embracing arm around an orange sunburst representing life. Like the name, the logo symbolized a new mission: "It is Herrick's purpose to prevent illness whenever possible, and to cure and heal whenever necessary. Herrick embraces life."

Timing was on Dunn's side as she sought and received approval for her plan, since she was able to show how the new wing and new name could work together to build visibility for the hospital if they were supported by a targeted public and media relations effort.

Once the changes were agreed to, new information materials and health-related programs were developed. The *Medical Staff News* became *Vita* (Latin for "life"). Employee newsletters were renamed *Pulse* and *Pulsebeats*. The community magazine *The Herricker* became a new quarterly tabloid called *Life*, with its circulation increased from 15,000 to 160,000 for almost the same cost because of a format change. Coupons in each issue offered a speakers bureau booklet and two new health education packages: the "life preserver" kit and "vial of life." The kit was designed to store preventive and practical health information. Actually a binder intended to be updated with new health tips included in each issue of *Life*, it came with telephone stickers, a first-aid fact sheet, Mr. Nasty comic strips to help deter children from household poisons, emergency information cards, personal medical history records and a home fire safety check list. The "vial of life" was designed for the ill or aged who have more frequent need for an ambulance or other emergency care. A sticker on the person's refrigerator door signaled the existence of a vial in the fridge. Within the vial a rolled-up sheet explained the owner's medical history, blood type, allergies and other relevant information invaluable to ambulance attendants if the person was unconscious.

To celebrate the completion of the new wing and use it to introduce "the new Herrick" to its many publics, Dunn arranged an 8-day open house. It involved a wide variety of health-related events aimed at internal and external audiences, including the media. News stories under headlines such as "A New Hospital for Berkeley" in that city's *Independent & Gazette*[1] and "Herrick Hospital An Innovator in Health Care" in the *Oakland Post*[2] provided wider exposure for the hospital's expanded health care services. The overall program generated positive feedback and unsolicited donations. It resulted in almost 6000 visitors to the new wing, some of whom had never been in the hospital before. It brought requests for hundreds of "life preserver" kits, "vials of life," and speakers bureau booklets—and a very personal response from one mailing recipient: "Congratulations. This is the best piece of junk mail I have ever received."

Dunn reflected on the role her department played not only in demonstrating their professional skills but also in contributing to the hospital's operations objectives: "I was very proud that the public relations program generated goodwill, greater visibility, and employee pride. But more than that, I was able to show the relationship between public and employee perceptions of the hospital and our results. There is nothing more rewarding to a public relations professional than to design and implement a public relations program that effects significant change."

Here are examples of other special events that have generated positive media coverage for both corporations and nonprofit organizations. They provide insight into how well-planned campaigns or events with an unusual twist can give an activity a unique enough angle that it becomes news in the eyes of editors and reporters:

CASE STUDIES

*Eager to shed its telephone company utility image, **AT&T Information Systems** co-sponsored the World Cup ski races in Aspen, Colorado in 1983, the first year of the company's existence as a separate subsidiary of AT&T, and established an annual award to recognize "an individual whose commitment to excellence and dedication to skiing has profoundly enriched the sport." The company's press kit carried no blatant sales pitch. In fact, it contained a great deal of information on Aspen's runs and skiing in general, and none at all on AT&T's products or services. It did include a background paper on why the company was creating a skiing award, with an explanation aimed at making it clear that AT&T's new subsidiary was ready to compete in the unregulated competitive marketplace: "One of the driving forces that keeps people skiing for life is the level of personal challenge, the taking of calculated risks, and the great physical and psychological rewards that result. We believe that those same driving forces are at work in the world of business. ... Today AT&T Information Systems is much like that racer in the starting gate ready to run a new race course. We are in a new business environment with all the knowledge and experience of AT&T behind us just as the racer faces his new challenge with years of practice and training at the ready."[3]*

***United Way** is a model of how nonprofit organizations can effectively use special events to generate positive publicity for their fund-raising efforts. Prominent CEOs always head up their campaigns. Not only does this tactic encourage increased corporate and employee giving but it also results in greater media attendance at speeches and press conferences as the CEO's prestige heightens the inherent news value. Overseas, the campaigns are similar but adapted to social and cultural differences. In Hong Kong, for example, small businesses employ more people than large corporations, so special events for the general public are more effective than organizational campaigns. In Japan, sumo wrestlers are the featured celebrities to draw media and public interest, rather than football players as in North America. And always the media are provided tools to make it easy for them to carry United Way news—from photographs and videotaped footage of children who will be helped by contributions to tours of agencies supported by United Way funds.[4]*

Western International Hotels took on a complex information job when it decided to change its name to **Westin Hotels**. *Now that it ran hotels all over the world, the company had outgrown the geographically limiting name that was created when almost all its facilities were in the State of Washington. Corporate officials and its agency, Cole & Weber, worked together to create all the materials necessary for a massive external and internal information campaign that was kicked off in January 1981. A presentation to the company's managers was followed by a major news conference with Chairman and CEO Harry Mullikin in Los Angeles. Information was simultaneously released over the nationwide Business Wire, and press kits were hand-delivered to key media in Seattle, Chicago, Los Angeles and New York. On a telephone cue, scaled down press packets were mailed to 1000 media contacts around the world. Public relations people at Westin's hotels in North America received copies of their packets on the same day as the Los Angeles news conference so they could make contact with local reporters and editors. At a media luncheon in New York City, journalists were given press kits and miniature bath towels carrying the new name, to capitalize on the advertising that was being launched in national and travel publications to announce the change. Altogether 55 hotels changed from Western International to Westin overnight. The company's press clippings analysis showed that word of the new name reached more than 78 million people in the first 3 months. In early 1982 research showed awareness of the new name had already topped 80% among frequent U.S. travelers.*[5]

Sometimes involving a celebrity can help promote an event. When Elizabeth Mitchell was publicizing a play, Disabled Genius, *produced by the* **Schwab Rehabilitation Center** *in Illinois, she had two tasks: to raise the profile of the center as well as promote the idea that disabled persons have many talents. The play starred actress Barbara Rush and a cast of disabled actors, both amateurs and professionals. Mitchell involved Joyce Sloane of "Second City" as chairwoman of her promotions planning committee. Sloane not only paved the way in the theatrical community but also provided name recognition for the play. Publicity began with the auditions and spread through PSAs, talk show interviews and a feature in the* Chicago Tribune.[6]

ALTERNATIVES TO SPECIAL EVENTS

There are times when special events are inappropriate. The hyped ceremony or the minor announcement masquerading as a major event reinforce the cynicism of journalists and the public, so you should follow the advice the Institute for Contemporary Studies offered President Ronald Reagan and use the news media "with selectivity and precision."[7] On occasion you will have the difficult task of talking your organization or client *out* of a major event like a news conference—and demonstrating how a targeted approach will more effectively meet the stated objectives even though it will not result in coverage in the *Wall Street Journal*.

David V. Manahan, whose media relations responsibilities for AT&T gave him wide experience in new product introductions, tells the story of the coal mine phone to illustrate this point. In the late 1970s Bell Labs developed an explosion-proof telephone for use in coal mines. It was the job of AT&T's marketing department to sell it, of course, so the product manager called a meeting to plan a marketing strategy and promotions program. He informed Manahan that he wanted to hold a news conference in New York City and would invite the *New York Times, Wall Street Journal, Business Week* and the three major television networks. "In my usual low-key manner I told him *I* would decide who we would invite to any news conference and where it would be held," Manahan chuckled. "Then I asked him who the customers were for this wonderful new system. His answer was coal mine superintendents." Coincidentally, Manahan had two sons in West Virginia and thus some acquaintances in the coal mining industry. He knew their work left little energy at the end of a long day for the *New York Times* and *Business Week*. Working with the product manager, he researched what they *did* read, and came up with a list of industry-specific publications like *Coal Age, Mining/ Processing Equipment*, and *Coal Industry News*. Manahan and his co-workers then took a map and some charts from a geography book to create a plastic overlay showing where coal mines were located in the United States. They came up with an eastern pocket including Virginia, West Virginia, Pennsylvania and Kentucky. The next step was to check trade show schedules for coal mine expositions, and they discovered one planned for Charleston, West Virginia. Space was quickly purchased and an exhibit constructed to display not only the coal mine phone but also other communications systems useful in the mining industry. Manahan booked the product manager on a press tour around West Virginia about a week before the trade show. "The coal mine phone is heavily insulated in a bright-orange cover," Manahan explained. "It looked like a big lunch box and it was very photogenic. During the interviews, we had the product manager stress the safety and productivity advantages of the phone—and show how its Touch-Tone dialing capability gave miners direct access to the outside world. No longer were they dependent on a switchboard operator who may or may not be there, depending on the shift."

The *Wall Street Journal* did not even know of this media activity, of course. But the personal demonstrations and the safety message resulted in wide coverage in newspapers and on television in the small communities of West Virginia. When the coal mining exposition was over the product manager had one firm sale, dozens of leads and news stories in the all-important trade press. "Some media relations purists view marketing promotions as hucksterism," Manahan said. "But product promotion can be as newsworthy as building a modern office complex or electing a new president—as long as you direct your messages to the right media. One of our responsibilities as media relations people must be to peddle our professionalism—and teach our associates what works and what does not work with the news media."

CASE STUDY

Creativity, like targeting, may provide an alternative to the big news conference. For example, an unusual giveaway can do as much for your program as a news conference if you are clever enough to think of one that is both unique and cost-effective. To promote the silver anniversary of its loader/backhoe, JI Case put together a breakfast press kit containing all the utensils and ingredients for a continental breakfast for two. The kit was delivered to reporters at 140 business and construction trade publications throughout the United States and Canada in a cardboard box marked "urgent." Included was a small cassette player providing a 4-minute message from Case's president. The cost of producing and sending these kits was one-third what it would have cost to hold a press conference for 140 media people, according to David Brukardt, manager of communications and public affairs at JI Case. Of the 140 publications receiving the kit, 38 responded with news coverage or personal letters to the company, and clips were still coming in 10 months after the event. Further, Brukardt thinks that the unusual and more personal nature of this promotion will help keep his company in journalists' minds longer than a normal press conference would.[8]

INGREDIENTS FOR PRESS KIT AT A SPECIAL NEWS EVENT

Regardless of whether you are announcing the purchase of property, dedicating a building, introducing a CEO or launching a new product, there are certain basic pieces that should be included in the package of materials you give the news media:

1. *Main news release.*
2. *Other related feature or "sidebar" stories.*
3. *Black-and-white photographs or drawings, with cutlines attached or taped to the back. Include color slides for TV. Offer color prints to magazines and newspapers with four-color capability, and offer network-quality videotape or film to TV stations as background footage if you have it.*
4. *List of names, titles and affiliations of all people on the stage, at the head table or otherwise participating in the event.*
5. *Photos and biographies of keynote speakers.*
6. *Basic fact sheet on your organization.*
7. *Annual report, brochure, and other information on your organization.*
8. *Name of person to contact for additional information.*

It also is critical that each of the pieces in the press kit be dated, since they undoubtedly will be separated and probably will be filed in the publication or station's morgue for future use by any reporter writing a story on your organization.

THE HIGH PRICE OF NEWS LEAKS

Frequently, employees are a major cause of news leaks. Sometimes they are salespeople hoping to impress customers by offering advance information about a new product, forgetting that they may be flirting with an antitrust violation by preannouncing a product. Or they are staff managers carelessly chattering about their work. Indeed, Business Week *explained how a major article on personal computers came to be written by quoting a reporter as saying, "I heard intimations at a lunch, at a cocktail party, and again from a research expert while I was in a grocery store about a major product announcement coming. Said publisher James R. Pierce candidly: "Using these bits of information as a wedge, [we] got interviews with [the company's] executives."*[9]

There is a very basic reason to keep a tight lid on new product information until the announcement day news conference: You likely cannot afford to alienate the news media and lose the free—and probably positive—publicity they will give you. Except in rare cases, journalists will not cover the announcement of a new product as a major news event if the story has leaked out in dribs and drabs. They understand the necessity for a trial location or two. But any more widespread knowledge and reporters tend to say too many of their readers or viewers already know the story to make it news—and they send you off to the very expensive advertising section. As the old saying goes, "Loose lips sink ships," or make it very expensive to float them again.

Editors also frequently refuse to carry a story on a new product on their news pages or programs if your company has a paid ad running. Their feeling is that if your company had time to produce and place an advertisement, the product is no longer "hard news" to their readers and viewers and they are being used to generate free advertising. It is thus an important part of the media relations person's responsibility to ensure your news conference precedes any advertising by at least several days.

TIPS FOR DEALING WITH INTERNATIONAL JOURNALISTS

Just when you think you have mastered the art of effectively serving U.S. journalists, suddenly your company or organization enters the international marketplace and you realize there is a whole new set of rules for media relations.

The first thing to do is to talk with someone knowledgeable in each country in which you are operating to find out how the media in that country operate. If you are starting from scratch and have no contacts at all, you might try the World Press Encyclopedia, *a two-volume reference work which discusses history, press laws, editorial policy and readership of more than 170 countries. Other sources include professional organizations such as the International Public Relations Association or the International Association of Business Communicators, each of whom may be able to give you names of contacts in your countries.*

The United States enjoys a freedom of the press virtually unmatched in any other country. So, it may come as a shock to find you have to deal with press clubs in Japan or a government-controlled media in another Far East country. The U.S. also has stringent libel laws which do not exist in other places. Understanding this will help ease the shock of reading stories about your company which have adjectives and adverbs of a completely negative and sometimes totally false nature.

If you deal extensively with non-U.S. media, you will run across other differences, as well:

1. *Business cards will vary in size from the format used in the U.S. to larger, 3″ × 5″ cards. Most will include the journalist's business and home addresses and telephone numbers, as well as telex and facsimile numbers. Many cards will be in the native language on one side and English on the other.*

2. *While the majority of international journalists speak English fluently, they often prefer the written material to be in their native language. This is important to remember when sending out press kits or preparing for international trade shows.*

3. *In many countries, the journalist you deal with is a lawyer or engineer first and a journalist second. This often means the difference between a general information interview and an in-depth, detailed kind of interview.*

4. *Photographs and slides are an essential ingredient in explaining to a non-U.S. journalist the operations, manufacturing, and marketing of a U.S. company.*

5. *"Pay for press" is a common practice among many non-U.S. media operations. In one form, this means paying the publication a "publishing fee" to have your release printed in the publication. In another, it can involve*

picking up the costs for a journalist to come to the U.S. for tours and interviews.

As you can tell, a lot of study and time is called for in order to make international media relations as successful as domestic.

CRISIS PLANNING

How to Anticipate and Manage
Emergency Situations

A new function called issues management has emerged in the field of public relations. It has come into being as a result of headlines that scream such emotional news as "Company Loses Discrimination Case" or "Workers Protest Unsafe Conditions" or "Buried PCBs Being Sought in Landfill." Coverage like this appears regularly in newspapers and on broadcasts all over the country. Although the copy in the full story often contains significantly less sensational language, those familiar with the issues might be forgiven if they long—like the judge who admonished a garrulous witness—for a little less heat and a lot more light. Reporters often provide only superficial, and sometimes emotional, coverage in disaster situations—as Robert MacNeil put it, "confident that the pundits or historians would sort out the context."[1] In turn, your objective in such "bad news" situations usually is clearly enunciated by the top management of your company or client: Make it go away. The question is how. Your role is to convince them that often the best way is to initiate contact with reporters—or, at the minimum, to respond promptly to questions—so your story is told once and for all. Bad news will not go away if you refuse to comment on it. In fact, lack of cooperation with the media may expand the story and make it last longer than if you handle the crisis and get it over with.

Issues management is not a science. After you strip away the fancy jargon you will find that much of what is called issues management is not really new at all. Until recently most public relations people—indeed, most managers—simply considered issues management to be a natural extension of good planning. Although there are times when we feel some personal inadequacy when events swirl beyond our reach, the feeling is not a modern phenomenon. Even Abraham Lincoln despaired: "I claim not to have controlled events, but confess plainly that events have controlled me," he wrote a year before the end of the American Civil War.[2] Still, thoughtful planning can help us to *not* be the guy running around stamping out ants and not seeing the elephants that are coming. Planning helps us meet scenarios that could be first-class media relations disasters with speed, professionalism, and at least the outward appearance of calm.

This chapter will cover crisis planning and media relations strategy as they relate to environmental affairs, equal opportunity, layoffs, accidents, and other situations that could develop into crises if not properly handled. We will cite case histories to show how media relations professionals actually managed critical issues communications. There is a danger in glamorizing examples in that they tend to mask the noteworthy nature of our routine, day-to-day activities; what professionals see as basic or even trivial situations can be considered extraordinary by a beginner. They are helpful, however, in helping us learn to apply the tools of our trade covered in earlier chapters. The principles, of course, are transferable to almost any subject—with some modification depending on whether the issue fundamentally concerns people, or is an economic or technological issue. First, we will talk about how to plan so that crises do *not* happen. Second, we will discuss how to handle crises when they *do* happen. (They will, in spite of the best planning, because you cannot control the elements, human nature or the outside world. The secret is to know what to do. Or, to paraphrase Rudyard Kipling, "How to keep your head when all about you are losing theirs.") Third, we will look at ways to get positive news into the media about your organization's efforts to deal with a critical issue or event.

Media relations people should be aware that news organizations also have crisis plans. CBS network news crews taped downtown and landmark scenes in Los Angeles in the summer of 1983 to update file video footage stored in New York that would be used in covering a major California earthquake. United Press International and at least two of the television networks maintain lists of southern California amateur radio operators to contact if phone communications with their Los Angeles bureaus are cut off.[3]

ENVIRONMENTAL ISSUES

Thoughtful planning is critical to all aspects of the media relations job, as we have pointed out previously. But nowhere is it more necessary than in the area of environmental affairs. Most of us will never find ourselves participating in the nightmare that faced the Hooker Chemical Company and its constituents at Love Canal, a landfill in Niagara Falls, New York, where leaks from a chemical waste dump prompted the evacuation of citizens' homes and their eventual purchase by the state in 1979.[4] However, a few barrels of waste shipped decades ago to a now-forgotten subcontractor running a disposal company can suddenly project you and your organization onto the front pages of the local newspaper and lead item on the six o'clock news—usually in a very negative context.

In the case of environmental issues, good planning begins with good teamwork and good communications among the public relations, engineering and legal people in your company or organization. If we restrict our thinking to stereotypical terms, the prospect of being a partner in a union of such diverse professions might prompt visions of discord, with the engineer insisting on a narrow, excessively logical approach; the lawyer intent on slotting acts into the black-and-white world of innocence or guilt; and the public relations person hiding the organization's sins behind a shield of "No comment." These stereotypes—if indeed they ever were built on the truths of some bygone era—do not exist in the reality of today for a variety of reasons, not the least of which is that none of these approaches works. On the contrary, the probing and questioning and desire to attack a problem from all angles unite the disciplines of engineering, law and communications in a unique synergism.

The Resource Conservation
and Recovery Act and Superfund

Before discussing methodologies, it is essential that the public
relations person have at least a basic understanding of some of the
key laws and regulations that cover the field of environmental
affairs. Two such major U.S. federal laws are the Resource
Conservation and Recovery Act (RCRA) and the Comprehensive
Environmental Response, Compensation and Liability Act
(CERCLA), better known by its nickname, Superfund. Even a
superficial look at these two acts makes it clear that the emphasis in
environmental control is shifting and the possibility of adverse
publicity for your organization in spite of its innocent intent is
rapidly increasing. A closer look can serve to make us aware of the
public relations ramifications of environmental legislation, and
what we as media relations professionals can do to help manage
such issues.

RCRA was enacted in 1976 to provide comprehensive regulation of wastes deemed hazardous to human health or the environment. It was designed to stop indiscriminate dumping of hazardous
wastes, close inadequate and dangerous landfills, stop other en-
vironmentally dangerous waste disposal practices, encourage recycling, and provide a mechanism for tracking hazardous wastes
"from cradle to grave." Since the law's passage, a maze of
regulations has been promulgated to ensure compliance. More
than 300 pages of regulations, explanations, and justifications were
published in the Federal Register in May 1980, putting RCRA into
effect in November 1980. Since then more than 40 amendments
have been issued. The interpretation and application of these
regulations is dynamic, with significant penalties for noncom-
pliance. Interpretations continue to be issued by the U.S. Environmental Protection Agency (EPA) and, often, by state
environmental agencies, which have primary responsibility for
implementing and enforcing the federal regulations and the option
of issuing more stringent limitations.

Any company or organization covered by the RCRA would do
well to have people intimately familiar with the specifics of the law,
including characterization of hazardous wastes, internal handling,
transportation requirements, disposal facility requirements, and
local and state regulations. The implications for public relations

became clear when it was apparent that not all disposal firms would be able to comply with the RCRA regulations for proper disposal of their customers' wastes. Because of the variability of site operations and the vulnerability of the sites' customers to improper disposal, responsible and forward-looking companies have evaluated disposal firms and developed a list of approved sites for disposal of hazardous wastes.

Liability of the sites' customers for past disposal of materials is not yet known. Companies and organizations have been using and disposing of significant quantities of chemicals for many years, and their wastes have been placed in hundreds of landfills throughout the United States. The unprecedented buy-out of the entire town of Times Beach, Missouri by the federal government in 1983 is but another manifestation of the power and the trauma of hazardous wastes. The town was literally dying of exposure to dioxin, a toxic chemical waste mixed with oil by a salvage dealer and spread on dirt roads and other areas in the early 1970s to keep down the dust.[5] Legal responsibilities for such cases will no doubt be established in the courtroom. But public opinion as to who is the culprit is likely to be determined by media coverage.

The EPA received its mandate from Congress to clean up hazardous waste sites from CERCLA, a broad law passed in 1980. More frequently known by the pot of money it created, the act started a "Superfund" of $1.6 billion. This money is to be used over 5 years to clean up some 400 waste sites nationwide. It is raised by a tax on chemical companies, with costs to be recouped from violators. EPA's enforcement role under Superfund is to ensure responsible party clean-up of sites and spills, and recovery from responsible parties of Superfund moneys spent. "Responsible party" includes the owner and/or operator of the site, the transporter if he selected the site, and the generator if he contracted with the owner or was negligent. Since EPA is empowered to collect damages equal to three times the government's clean-up costs—from one company or from any combination of the responsible parties—there is built-in incentive for responsible-party sponsored clean-up so they can manage the effort themselves and thus control the costs.

EPA's first assignment under Superfund was to identify abandoned and hazardous disposal sites. By mid-1981, any person who owned or operated a facility that treated, stored or disposed of

hazardous waste was required to have notified EPA of the existence of the facility. EPA received 9200 such notifications. On
October 31, 1981 EPA published a list of 115 waste sites scheduled
for priority clean-up under Superfund. That figure subsequently
grew to 418. The agency is negotiating settlements with those
responsible for wastes at the sites—but many people have criticized EPA for moving excessively slowly on clean-up efforts. On
top of such complaints, the public uproar in early 1983 over EPA's
effectiveness resulted in top agency personnel being dismissed and
Congressional investigations into destruction of documents and
fraternization with regulated companies. This shows that environmental hazards represent a volatile political—and media—issue.[6]
Indeed, pollster Lou Harris says that environmental protection
"happens to be one of the sacred cows of the American public."[7]

BASIC PREPAREDNESS

From both a legal and public relations viewpoint, the most
significant aspect of Superfund is that fault does not seem to
matter. With the best of intentions your company or organization
could have contracted decades ago with a trucker or a landfill
owner to dispose of waste that was considered nothing more than
unneeded garbage. Yet tomorrow your organization could be
hearing from the EPA about a long-forgotten landfill on which
barrels with your logo and traces of hazardous substances have
been found. A few hours later your phone could ring, with a
reporter on the other end of the line—on deadline and asking you
for a statement. So the first thing you might want to do after
reading this section is find out if your organization is covered by
RCRA, Superfund, or other such environmental legislation. If so,
an immediate planning session with your legal and engineering
colleagues is in order. As public relations people you can do a
much better job for your organizations when you know about
potential problems in advance. Talk about the *facts* of the situation. And also talk about how the public might *perceive* the
situation. In a crisis involving a gut issue like environmental
pollution, reality and perception often can be two different things.

Second, decide who will be the spokesperson in the issue if a
reporter calls. As emphasized in Chapter 5, whoever it is should

know the facts very well and be able to tell the company's story confidently and positively. Each organization will have its own reasons for deciding who should be the spokesperson—and the designation may change depending on the topic. The key is to decide ahead of time, before the crisis hits.

Third, work together on a stand-by statement, expected reporter questions, and proposed answers. With this effort, you have probably accomplished the most important goal of all: You are all ready for a reporter's call. If and when a reporter does call, you should make a quick check with the appropriate person in the organization to be sure you have the latest information. Then you should promptly and confidently call the reporter back and answer the questions. In any case, you will have avoided a crisis— assuming you view a crisis, as most people do, as an emotion-charged event characterized by hand-wringing, awkward silences, and confusion about what to do next.

Preparedness is not self-sustaining, however. It takes ongoing contact between you and the appropriate people in your organization so that you can continue to anticipate future issues and do the advance work necessary to keep them from erupting into public problems. Public relations programs can be valuable operations tools. But you are not a miracle worker. Too often public relations programs are based on impossible dreams. You should not be expected to keep all the bad news out of the paper or off the television screen. The vast majority of all reporters are professionals who want to do the complete job. They know there are at least two sides to every news story, they want to get the complete picture, and they are more than willing to include your position in their report. Their hearing the full story on such potentially emotional issues as a poorly maintained landfill often results in your turning what could have been a negative article into a neutral or a balanced one.

Public relations people should ideally be brought into the act well before all of the decisions are made on a sensitive environmental issue. The critical counselor role of the public relations professional is covered in depth in Chapter 10. But it bears repeating here and in virtually every chamber where decision makers gather to discuss actions that will affect one of their many publics. If PR people are but privates in an army of generals, some of their most valuable skills are lost to their organizations. As CNN

Headline News Anchor Bobby Batiste put it: "The public relations person is more important than anyone else in the organization as far as we are concerned—and should be briefed accordingly." Public relations people often can counsel their operations and staff colleagues on how the public might perceive a planned action. Working together, you can avoid many problems. Sometimes that may require modifying an action plan to demonstrate your organization's commitment to environmental protection. Good relations with the public are, after all, based on a solid record of good performance. Many times it will require developing a communications program to explain your plans internally and externally.

THE BRIGHTER SIDE OF BUILDING CREDIBILITY

It would be a disservice to all public relations people to end a discussion of environmental affairs after reviewing only the negative aspects of the topic. On the contrary, we much prefer to work on positive news.

Reporters—particularly on the smaller newspapers and stations—are often looking for good feature material and information that affect their readers or viewers. Offering them story ideas helps them do their jobs better—and is an excellent vehicle by which you can get to know them. They will come to respect you as news sources, and are much more likely to check in with you on any news affecting your organization if you have worked with them before. Also, there is a plus on a personal level for PR people. When you are responding, it is often to bad news. When you are initiating, it is often to "sell" good news. Obviously, it is much more fun to be in the initiative mode. Energy and environmental issues *are* news these days. In spite of what we may think on occasion, reporters want to cover good news as well as bad.

AT&T's manufacturing subsidiary has been successful at placing news of its energy conservation efforts with the trade and technical press that cover both the telecommunications and the environmental industries as well as the general media in towns where the company operates. For example, each year since the first OPEC oil shock in 1973 prompted a concerted conservation effort, the company has issued an annual energy usage report giving overall corporate results and citing the best efforts of its hundreds of facilities—factories, office buildings, service centers, and warehouses—around the United States. A national news release on this report results in coverage in the trade press. It also provides offices around the country with a pattern release they can adapt by featuring their facility's results and quoting their local manager. For locations which won awards in the conservation contest, the lead becomes obvious and can result in positive headlines like, "Western Conservation Drive Cuts Light Bill by $91,000."[8]

If your company or client has recycling efforts underway, they provide fine opportunities for news releases—and also excellent "before and after" photo opportunities—in these resource-conscious times. As an example, a feature on recycling the excess plastic left over from the molding process used in manufacturing telephones resulted in a lengthy feature in the trade publication *Design News* under the headline, "Recycling Plastic Trash into Treasure"[9] and in *Telephony*,[10] one of the leading magazines covering the communications industry. Because of the dramatic photo and catchy subhead, "Raking It In," the photograph ran in a wide variety of newspapers across the country ranging from the *Lexington* (Kentucky) *Leader*[11] to the *Phoenix* (Arizona) *Gazette*.[12] All included the fact that the plant had the biggest and most efficient plastics in-plant reclamation system in the United States.

This positive—and almost priceless—press coverage resulted from company-initiated news releases. Often equally fine results come from responding promptly and factually to a reporter's request to you—as we did to a call from *Electronic Engineering Times* asking if we would like to participate in a series of columns featuring chief executive officers of leading U.S. companies. The resulting article, "Energy Conservation as Corporate Policy," was carried by the publication in June 1981[13] and later reprinted in a special booklet that was a fine handout for subsequent media and community contacts.

These articles are not merely corporate puffery. To make the news pages, your story has to have a news angle. You must be the biggest, the best, or some other superlative. Your news must be unique enough to be of interest to others in the industry or important enough to be of interest to the general public.

Organizations and companies involved in disputes over landfills, oil spills, air and water pollution, or other negative environmental issues will settle their criminal and civil liability in courtrooms. The monetary stakes admittedly are high. Even so, they are likely to be less damaging in the long run than the public's belief that your organization is unconcerned about protecting the environment or managing its resources. It is for this reason that you need an ongoing effort to tell your positive environment stories to the public via the media. You have to build a base of credibility to stand on if negative news forces you to implement that crisis contingency plan you developed.

Although it is unwise to become preoccupied with counting press clippings and radio or TV mentions, they are one important measure for the simple reason that they indicate how often you are getting your message—in this case a positive environmental message—out to the public. It is an accepted fact from advertising research that you have to expose your message to your audience over and over again before it is remembered for any length of time.

AT&T's found itself in a situation with its Nassau Recycle Corporation subsidiary which caused us to wonder if we would use up every drop of goodwill our previous media relations efforts had generated. In March of 1982, polychlorinated biphenyl (PCB) contaminants were found at the South Carolina facility. AT&T immediately shut down the offending operation for a brief period until it was cleaned up, took additional steps to ensure that the companies dealing with the facility knew PCBs had to be separated out before scrap was shipped to Nassau for recycling since it is not equipped to handle them, paid a fine, and answered reporters' questions honestly and factually. Those of us handling the media relations were satisfied that the resultant press coverage was balanced. Actually, it was very fair considering the emotions that news of PCBs tends to generate.

Then the unthinkable happened: A neighbor's cows died and he publicly blamed Nassau. The engineers assured us the company could not be at fault. But we had to wait for government-sponsored tests by outside experts to prove our innocence. As we waited, we read the headlines: "Cows' Deaths Have Residents Suspicious," and "Thirty-eight Cows Die; DHEC Alerted." It was a little like watching a horror show—the monster is so terrifying you find it hard to convince yourself life will return to normal as soon as the film is over and the lights come up. A month and a half later we got the clearance the engineers had promised.

Headlines dutifully reported, "Nassau Contamination Not Causing Cows to Die, Test Results Indicate" and "Nassau Plant Cleared in Probe."[14]

It is impossible to know, of course, how many people read of the cows' deaths and then missed the headlines telling of the company's innocence. But throughout it was some consolation that the media consistently included our statements in their reports, and that we previously had been given extensive coverage of Nassau's leading-edge recycling efforts in those same papers. In a situation like this you want to guard against overreacting to coverage of your bad news. Do not be like the parishioners who caused their preacher to chide: "We use our religion like a trolley car—we ride it only when it is going our way."

NUCLEAR ENERGY AS NEWS

Nuclear energy is another controversial environmental issue that tends to generate dramatic headlines and lengthy news coverage. In 1975, when Seattle-First National Bank was named bond fund trustee for a new issue of state power system bonds, its officers had no idea that this action would result in the bank's becoming the center of a nuclear controversy. Yet as events unfolded, the move eventually appeared to put the bank in the position of defending massive cost overruns at a nuclear power plant construction site and supporting increased electrical costs for Washington State consumers. Further, the controversy threatened to disrupt the bank's annual meeting and affect profits as customers withdrew deposits and closed their accounts. It was contained with a quickly conceived but well-thought-out public information program in which bank executives' face-to-face meetings with selected media representatives were an integral part of a successful strategy.

Like any full-service bank, Seafirst routinely assists corporations and public agencies when they issue bonds. In 1975 the bank was low bidder among several major banks for trusteeship of Washington Public Power Supply System's (WPPSS) Project 3 bonds, to be used to build a new nuclear plant. (These bonds are different from the issue that made headlines in 1983 when it became by far the largest municipal bond default in U.S. history.) The bond resolution defining the trustee's responsibilities for this project was not unusual: It was to monitor the issues' compliance with the terms of the bond resolution and take whatever actions appropriate on behalf of the bondholders; and to administer debt service, including payments of principal and interest, to bondholders. The phrase "whatever action appropriate on behalf of the bondholders" is standard to such agreements, so it aroused no undue anxiety in the minds of the bank's officers signing the contract. It would have taken a soothsayer to know back then that the letters "WPPSS" sound suspiciously like "whoops" when turned into an acronym and said aloud.

The first signs of trouble occurred when Initiative 394 generated enough support to appear on the November 1981 ballot in Washington State. The measure required elections before additional bonds could be issued on such big energy projects as WPPSS nuclear plants, which were experiencing huge cost overruns. In effect, its supporters pointed out, it gave consumers the right to vote before they would be required to finance expensive nuclear power plants. Thus they would have some control over rising electric bills that carry the financing costs. It was a powerful argument, and the initiative passed. Seafirst officers and lawyers conferred among themselves and with two other banks which served as trustees for bondholders at other WPPSS sites. The result was a public relations problem of the highest order: The three banks took legal action to overturn Initiative 394. Bank officials said they had no choice. Indeed, they argued, they had a moral and legal obligation to file suit against the initiative, and Seafirst would have left itself open to a lawsuit by angry bondholders if it did not act. The bank pointed out that as a result of the initiative, two other nuclear projects had been terminated and their bond ratings suspended.

Public reaction was swift and pointed, led by a new activist movement called Irate Ratepayers which recruited members throughout the state. Thousands of consumers gathered at Public Utility District meetings to demand explanations from their commissioners. Citizens and politicians called for a boycott of Seafirst, and some branches experienced pickets and account withdrawals. The Irate Ratepayers groups set April 1 as "draw day" and generated wide publicity to encourage Seafirst customers to join together and close their accounts that day.

When the bank filed its lawsuit in December 1981, its top two public relations positions were vacant, and the PR department was given no advance warning. So it was behind from the start. The PR people's greatest efforts initially were focused internally—to explain the bank's complicated position to staff via normal media while at the same time educating top management to the severity of the situation. Many executives thought the problem would go away. But it got bigger and bigger. The Irate Ratepayers were front-page news around the state as they brought their demands to various Seafirst branches, held impromptu news conferences at the bank's facilities and hosted statewide meetings with press conferences afterwards. Seafirst's media relations people were busy "fighting fires"—responding to questions from scores of reporters around Washington State.

Clearly, the bank needed a broad plan to aggressively tell its side of the story. They developed a multifaceted information program to reach their customers, employees, and the general public via a variety of means, ranging from internal bulletins and special teller briefings to newspaper advertisements and information sheets prominently displayed in branches. Integral to the plan was a media visitation program. "It was obvious that there was wide confusion and misinterpretation about the bank's involvement in the lawsuit," said Arthur P. Merrick, Seafirst's vice president and manager of corporate communications. "The Irate Ratepayers had a consumer-oriented message that was getting a great deal of media coverage. We needed to use our top people to tell *our* side to the media—and get our position out to a wider external audience, particularly our customers, who were being told to withdraw their money from the bank."

The strategy was to send a small group of senior executives from the bank to major television stations and newspapers to explain the bank's position. Primary focus was on reaching news directors and assignment editors, editorialists and commentators, business editors and reporters, labor writers, energy writers, and city editors. Influential journalists were identified by name as key contacts. Individual meetings were arranged by the corporate communications department but held at the papers' and stations' offices, not at the bank, to make it easier for as many editors and reporters as possible to attend. They were scheduled to occur before April 1, "draw day." Their message was threefold: That claims were being made about Seafirst and its policies that were generating unusually high media attention; that the bank executives wanted to lay their facts and positions on the table to ensure accurate treatment of the bank in ensuing stories; and that although the bank was not seeking coverage of this meeting in particular, it would welcome contact from reporters whenever they were writing stories on these issues. In addition, the spokespersons were prepared to answer questions on other subjects that Merrick's media relations staff thought might come up during the meetings. The sessions were informal, emceed by a public relations senior executive, and usually lasted about an hour. Questioning was tough and probing.

Almost immediately there was a noticeable change in the thrust of media coverage on the issue. Headlines like "Energy Rebels Taking Aim at Seafirst"[15] and "Irate Ratepayers Urge Boycott of Seafirst Over Nuclear Bond Issue"[16] changed to "Seafirst Says it's Getting a Raw Deal"[17] and "Seafirst Caught in the Middle."[18] Opined the *Seattle Post-Intelligencer* in an editorial appearing the morning before "draw day": "Seattle-First National Bank, through no fault of its own, is caught between the proverbial rock and a hard place...If Seafirst failed to challenge the initiative, the bank convincingly observes, bondholders could make a legal case against Seafirst for neglecting its responsibility as trustee to seek protection of their interests. ... The net result of Seafirst's uncomfortable trustee position is that it has incurred the wrath of the state's rapidly mobilizing irate electrical ratepayers and the bank has become a convenient target for their anger at the documented financial profligacy of WPPSS. ... Such action in the *P-I's* view, while understandable, is unfair to Seafirst, which in the final analysis is as much a victim of WPPSS mismanagement as the state's ratepayers ... "[19]

This turnaround in media coverage demonstrates once again the fact that most journalists want to include both sides of an issue in their stories. They will support your organization editorially if you have convincing arguments. Where corporate America's leaders in particular often go wrong is in not going to the media with their views—and then criticizing the resultant media coverage as being unfair or inaccurate. The power of the press and bottom-line benefits to the organization of supportive external news coverage are also demonstrated by this Seafirst case. Only 341 people responded to the calls to pull money out of the bank on "draw day" and only $640,000 was withdrawn—about a penny and a half for every $1000 on deposit at the bank.

Merrick offered several tips to others involved in similar situations. "First of all, get management and staff on your side and get them involved in telling your story," he said. "We did that in the branches—we even had branch managers writing articles for the op-ed pages of their local newspapers. And we used our executives in talking to the media. It humanized us as an institution in a tough spot. It is also critical to plan—jointly with the operating departments—on a worst-case basis. We worked together on security precautions, cash reserves for any large runs on branches, reporting processes so we could provide accurate data to the media on a same-day basis, plus internal and external communications." And from a media relations perspective? "Be aggressive with the media when it serves your cause," he advised. "We fought the battle for the headlines on 'draw day' and we won. We knew we had to frame the stories on our terms, so we called it 'a fizzle and flop.' The other side said it was 'just a beginning.' But our words prevailed—or at worst, got equal treatment. Clearly you don't have to say 'no comment' about a case that's in litigation. In no way did we do or say anything that jeopardized our legal position." Not only did Seafirst's active information effort turn around public opinion, it also made a direct contribution to the bank's business results. "We actually had many people come in to our branches to open accounts as a result of our strong stand on behalf of our bondholder customers," Merrick said.

EQUAL EMPLOYMENT ISSUES

Another emotional issue that can become a media crisis is equal employment opportunity. Many organizations find out the hard way—through expensive litigation and well-publicized court cases—that it is almost as important to spend time ensuring the local community is *aware* of your affirmative efforts in the field of EEO as it is to actually implement your programs.

For the community to believe you are truly an equal opportunity employer, it is essential that the local media reflect that position in their coverage of your organization—or at the minimum, not negate it.

The concept of equal opportunity is not a new one, but its emphasis has changed over the years. During the 1960s, recruiting efforts and special training programs were principally concerned with fulfilling the most urgent need of the times—providing more entry-level jobs for blacks and other minorities. With success, social and business customs changed—and people's expectations and aspirations expanded. The focus shifted in the 1970s to providing greater opportunities for qualified women and minority group members to progress in their companies or agencies to positions of greater responsibility and influence, and to establishing programs for handicapped employees and veterans. In the 1980s, stress on numerical quotas as ends in themselves is diminishing as affirmative action becomes a matter of business routine and solid progress is made at ensuring every qualified applicant has a fair shot at any job—be it a woman aspiring to be a police officer, a man desiring to be a secretary, or a minority aiming for the next promotion up the management ladder.

Equally sensitive, and more subtle, aspects of the EEO issue are surfacing and demanding resolution. The equal-pay-for-comparable-work issue has developed because women continue to earn significantly less than men. Its proponents cite as evidence of systematic discrimination the fact that jobs traditionally held by women—for example, nurses—are routinely paid less than those dominated by men—such as electricians. This so-called comparable worth issue is attracting Congressional attention and judicial rulings—and thus, media attention as well. There is also a new emphasis on age discrimination, although the law covering this issue goes back to 1967 and the Age Discrimination in Employment Act. This law is unusual in that it mandates a jury trial, which greatly increases the odds of wider publicity and media coverage. The trend toward raising or eliminating the mandatory retirement age has resulted in an increase in older employees on the payroll. Also, the American labor force is aging. In 1979, 16.7% of the population in the United States was 40 years old or older; the U.S. Bureau of the Census predicts that 30 years from now that percentage will soar to 45.5% of the population.[20] Similar trends toward a greater number of older employees exist in Canada, Great Britain, and Europe. A recessionary economy such as that experienced in the early 1980s adds a double-edged sword by making it more urgent than ever for employers to trim payrolls—and for employees to hold on to their jobs as long as possible.

Sexual harassment is another current EEO issue. Defined under Title VII of the U.S. Civil Rights Act of 1964, guidelines issued in November 1980 and administered by the Equal Employment Opportunity Commission make an employer liable for employees who are guilty of sexual harassment, since they say employers have an affirmative duty to prevent it from occurring. These regulations make clear that harassment is illegal not only when a woman loses her job or is denied a promotion but also when sexual harassment creates an "intimidating, hostile, or offensive working environment." Similar laws exist in Canada, where the subject is also getting publicity. Indeed, about 1.2 million Canadian women and 300,000 men believe they have been sexually harassed, according to projections in a Canadian Human Rights Commission survey. The figures mean 15% of Canadian women and 4% of Canadian men have at some time had an experience they felt was sexual harassment.[21] Yet another recent entry into the world of equal opportunity is an organization's maternity benefits policy—and, once the baby is born, its child-care practice for both mothers and fathers (the latter dubbed "paternity leaves" by the ever label-hungry media).

These types of cases make good copy from a journalist's perspective because they have a strong human interest factor. They can be particularly troubling from the organization's viewpoint not just because they are intrinsic "no win" situations but also because they tend to take years to resolve and each stage in the litigation offers the possibility of another news story. How your organization is portrayed by the media if such cases become local public issues will depend to a great extent on three factors: First, whether the reporter knows who you are and how to reach you so that your organization's position is carried in the story (proof that establishing ongoing relationships with local reporters is a must); second, what type of previous coverage the publication's or station's files reveal your organization received on equal opportunity issues (reporters are usually in a hurry, so when they check the morgue or library you want to be sure they get accurate facts—the key reason for asking for a correction on the file copy if there is a significant error in any news coverage); and third, the general feeling that reporter has about your organization (a highly subjective reaction that could be based on such a substantive rationale as several interviews with your CEO and detailed knowledge of your product line, or formed merely from casual conversations with employees who are neighbors or being held up by traffic each morning as your workers turn left at a busy intersection).

When an equal opportunity case is filed against your organization, the same type of advance alerts and close communication discussed for environmental issues are essential for you to do your job—only this time your teammates are legal and personnel experts. You need to be informed of the existence of any such cases, be they informal complaints to the local Equal Employment Opportunity Commission or formal suits in a court of law. You need a copy of the plaintiff's complaint and your organization's reply when it is filed, since these are matters of public record. It buys you a great deal in relations with the news media to cooperate by providing such public information materials to key reporters, and the payback is usually more accurate coverage and an enunciation in the story of your organization's position.

Almost inevitably, the first time you check with your organization's lawyer before responding to a journalist's query on a case such as an EEO complaint the immediate response will be to have no comment at all while the case is in litigation. "We will try this suit in the courtroom, not on the front page of the newspaper" is often the pompous response. This position is dangerous, for it ignores the fact that the court of public opinion will indeed rule on your case whether or not you approve—and whether or not your organization's position is included in the evidence before it. How much more satisfactory to your employer or client, the reporter and the public to have a plan agreed to in advance that meets each of these constituencies' needs.

One complicating factor is that often a reporter hears word of a suit before you do and is clamoring for a response on a very short deadline. Do not be content to issue a standard "We have not seen a copy of the complaint and thus cannot comment" reply. Many readers or viewers will take that to be an expression of guilt because your organization did not take the opportunity to defend itself. You may never get another chance to tell your side of the story to the public. Rather, answer such a request for comment by first positively stating your commitment to equal opportunity and citing some concrete results—and only later responding to the specific suit. For example, if an employee charges your organization with discrimination based on her sex, and your lawyer either has not yet received a copy of the complaint or filed your response, a stand-by statement you should have cleared and ready to give reporters might read: "The Jones Manufacturing Company is committed to equal opportunity for women—and our record of hiring and promoting women proves that. Last year almost half of the promotions in our company were earned by women. Women are actively involved in training programs we sponsor to help them expand their technical and management skills. We have not yet received a copy of the suit which you refer to [or, We are currently investigating this specific complaint]. But we are confident our equal opportunity record will hold up well under any objective review."

Be sure your lawyer gives you a copy of the legal reply once it is filed in court. It is a valuable document in that it affirmatively enunciates your organization's defense to each of the specific charges. It is a public document once filed, so there should be no objection to your using information from it if a reporter calls.

If an EEO case goes to trial, you will want to be prepared with a statement previously cleared by your legal and personnel people that briefly states your position—again taken from the official papers your lawyer has filed with the court. Be sure it includes a positive "quotable quote" in the first one or two paragraphs—and saves legal and other background information for later in the story—so that even the tightest editing by the broadcast media does not eliminate your main point. Whether you choose to be in the courtroom to personally hand out the statement, issue a news release including it, or merely have it handy to reply if reporters call in with questions will depend on the severity of the case and your judgment as to whether or not the media will cover the trial in person. Often your being in court adds a significance you do not wish to give the suit. As long as you are comfortable that reporters know how to reach you, you often are better off operating in a "business as usual" mode from your office—with the stand-by statement handy in case it is needed.

If your organization decides to settle an equal opportunity suit rather than let it go to trial, you also will want to weigh the pros and cons of initiative versus responsive courses of action to let the news out. If the case had pretrial publicity, or the plaintiff or other lawyer has a practice of going to the press with their version, you may want to issue a news release—or at least call a few key reporters and the local wire service bureaus if the case has drawn statewide or nationwide attention—to ensure your organization's statement is carried in any story. If the case were not widely known, you may be better off merely being prepared to answer media queries. In any event, your statement in a settlement should enunciate your organization's commitment to equal opportunity and perhaps include something like "We settled this case so we could devote our energies to continuing to work on equal opportunity programs at the Smith Association, rather than waste our resources in a nonproductive effort like a trial. Much has been accomplished—but much more needs to be done." Thus you have not admitted guilt and you have neutralized a negative story and used it as a platform for a positive message.

Responding to difficult queries and combating negative press is like assuming command of the troops when the battle is nearly lost. Fortunately, however, there are times when you can mount a major offensive and move positively into news rooms armed with an arsenal that will stop the fire—at least temporarily. On an ongoing basis, there are many practices you can integrate into your media relations programs to specifically and positively influence journalists'—and through them, the public's—views of your organization's equal opportunity track record.

1. Look for ways to publicize the upward movement of women and minorities in your organization by issuing news releases on their promotions or significant achievements to their community papers, professional or technical publications, alumni association or minority publications in your area. They make good feature stories for editors who usually welcome "home town person makes good" material, they provide role models for younger readers or viewers who have not yet chosen career paths (or need positive reinforcement if they have), and they demonstrate that your organization has more than a "paper" commitment to equal opportunity.

2. Review your news release distribution lists to be sure they include media geared to minorities and women. Translate releases and radio tapes into Spanish or another language if you have significant foreign language media in your area.

3. Look for opportunities to use women or minorities as spokespersons for your organization. Issue news releases when they give public talks to local clubs or associations.

4. Try to interest feature writers in stories on your employees

taking leadership roles in minority organizations like the Urban League or United Negro College Fund, professional or technical conferences such as "women in engineering" days, or unique working mothers' child-care activities.

5. Issue news releases and invite reporters to attend if your organization participates in minority supplier fairs or career days. Write feature stories on minority businesses with whom you have signed supplier or distributor contracts.

6. Take a look at the brochures you distribute or films you show to external and internal audiences to see if they demonstrate—or conflict with—your organization's claim to supporting equal opportunity. All of these materials should be visual ambassadors for your organization and its employment practices. If your employment advertisements carry the tagline "An equal opportunity employer" but the brochure you give a reporter carries photographs of women only in traditionally female jobs and white males only in management roles or historically male disciplines like engineering, the journalist is likely to question your company or client's sincerity. From a jaundiced reporter on a slow news day, this disparity could even result in a feature story along the lines of "Jones Shoe Company Claimed EEO Policy but Internal Documents Show Actual Practice Different."

7. Conversely, do not use set-up pictures for news photos or your organization's other materials that could be misleading. To imply that you have the "perfect" employment mix in all levels of your organization by taking a photograph of several women and minorities in a boardroom situation, for example, is phony—and might result in even more negative reaction. It is equally important to not leave the impression by showing only women or minorities that reverse discrimination is inevitable.

8. Review your material as a sensitized person might interpret it, to guard against inferred discrimination. If an attractive woman is posing with a new product, be sure there is a concrete purpose to having her in the picture—a much stronger reason than just to attract attention in a "cheesecake" manner. If your CEO is giving a recruiting speech to a university class, be sure it does not call for "young, aggressive managers" to join the business. Make it simply "aggressive managers." If you are writing a news release, avoid characterizing executives, decision makers, or even customers as "he" while speaking of secretaries and clerical

workers as "she." Few businesses can afford to alienate women who might be offended by such stereotyping, albeit inadvertent. Better to avoid the individual pronoun altogether by using the plural—or use the affirmative "he or she," which has become so common it is no longer awkward in most situations.

Reporters also are making special attempts to avoid biased communications that might unintentionally offend readers or viewers. Indeed, the media's own stylebooks have been updated to carry anti-stereotyping advice down to details such as eliminating descriptions of the hobbies, number of children and shoe color of women presidents unless such homey touches also would be included in stories of male leaders. Recently an editor in New England apologized in print for the use of the phrase "deaf and dumb" in a news story: "We realize now the terminology did a great deal of damage and we will live uncomfortably with that fact ... though the mistake was inadvertant and without malice," editor William Ketter wrote in the *Patriot Ledger* in a message to his readers. "We regret it and promise to learn from the experience. We do not take lightly our obligation to print the news with good taste, common sense, and with proper attention to human dignity."[22]

A strong desire to avoid offending current and potential employees, customers, shareowners, clients, or suppliers is reason enough for most organizations to pay careful attention to the words and tone of their communications. In addition, there is a federal law in the United States relating to such efforts. In December 1971, a new regulation was issued to apply to all companies that work for the U.S. federal government either directly as suppliers or indirectly as subcontractors. Called Revised Order No. 4, the law's best-known provisions set numerical goals and timetables for companies to meet in employment matters. Its communications section included two rules of specific interest to public relations people: "When employees are featured in advertising, employee handbooks or similar publications, both minority and nonminority men and women should be pictured"; and, "When recruiting brochures pictorially present work situations, the minority and female members of the work force should be included." At least one company recognized the far-reaching implications of this new law. Pacific Northwest Bell gave one of its managers the special

assignment for 6 months in 1972 of reviewing all its corporate information pieces and training its managers on how to bring communications materials into compliance with the forward-looking
provisions of Revised Order No. 4. This unusual effort made it
clear the company was dedicated to carrying out the letter and the
spirit of the equal opportunity laws and regulations. It also helped
ensure the many printed and audiovisual materials Pacific Northwest Bell produced for internal and external audiences, including
the news media, avoided even a hint of inadvertant typecasting of
particular kinds of people into particular jobs.

EMPLOYEE LAYOFFS

Employee layoffs represent another sensitive issue that can result
in either negative news coverage or straight matter-of-fact reporting depending upon how well you are prepared to explain your
actions to reporters. Once again, careful planning and good
relationships with the media are the keys to your success. Because
people's lives and self-esteem are so directly involved, this subject
calls for keen sensitivity on the part of corporate spokespersons.

　　Here again you will need to decide whether you should issue a
news release or merely respond to reporters' questions. If there
are only a few people involved, relatively speaking—say, 40 or 50
out of a work force of several thousand—no release may be
necessary. But if reporters have been calling to ask the status of
your employment situation, or if this layoff is the second or third in
a series that the media and the community might perceive as a
pattern requiring further explanation, you will probably feel you
should distribute a news release or at least phone major reporters
with the facts. Often initiating contacts with the media in an
essentially negative situation can result in the reporter's making a
special point to carry your position—and even turn a negative story
into a positive one.

　　In either case, a written piece—be it a news release or a
background statement—is a must. Questions and answers are
advisable also—not only for your use but also for local managers
who could get queries from reporters calling for an on-the-scene
reaction and almost certainly will be questioned by their employees and neighbors. It is essential in handling any critical issue

that all spokespersons for your organization "sing from the same song sheet"—that is, enunciate the same facts, rationale and tone whether they are talking to workers, union representatives, civic leaders or reporters.

To facilitate such consistency, if you work for a national or international organization, it is wise to keep track of all locations' layoffs at headquarters and share that information with local spokespersons who are putting together information materials before a layoff announcement. Reporters often want to know if the problems are isolated to your immediate area or part of a bigger picture. You also may want to prepare a general statement that can be used as a pattern piece by all your locations. You should advise other facilities whenever one is going to release news of a significant layoff in case that announcement generates queries from their local media.

When you are putting together Qs and As in a layoff situation, think of the kinds of questions your spouse or friends would ask if you went home and told them the news: How many people? How long have they worked for the company? What types of jobs are involved? Why did you lay them off? What did you do to try to avoid this layoff? What chances do they have of getting hired back? And the inevitable, do you think there will be more layoffs in the future? Reporters ask the same types of questions any interested person would. Your ability to answer them promptly, candidly, in human terms, and in simple English (rather than corporate bafflegab) will do much to contribute to objective media coverage. An example of a down-to-earth answer to the difficult question of what the future holds was given by AT&T spokesman Dick Birkmeyer, who was quoted in the Baltimore *News American* at the time of a layoff in 1980: "I hate to give people false hopes, and yet I don't want to paint a 'gloom and doom' picture. It's just that we don't know what's going to happen. We're the last ones who would be sitting here with a crystal ball. We hope the national economy won't deteriorate further and impact on us . . ."[23]

Look for ways to stress your organization's concern for the laid off workers and their families. Are you offering extended medical insurance coverage, for example? Or termination allowances, career counseling, education and training assistance, or relocation aid?

It also is critical that you be intimately familiar with the provisions of the contract if your employees are represented by a union. Labor negotiations are much like international diplomacy— words and phrases that sound innocuous can have any special meanings to those involved. For example, citing advances in technology or the introduction of robots on the factory floor as one of the reasons for a layoff could result in your organization having to make a special severance payment to affected workers, depending on the provisions of their contract. Gain the confidence of those responsible for labor relations for your company or client before a layoff is imminent. Have them review your proposed news release, statement, and answers well before you need to use them. Ask them to alert you in advance to any sensitive or negative issue a disgruntled worker could plant with a reporter so that you can work together on an appropriate response.

It is also important to get everyone's agreement in advance to a detailed announcement timetable. Your labor relations people likely will want to privately inform national and local union leaders a day or so in advance. If the layoff is a major one, your CEO also may want to alert the mayor, legislators, or other key community leaders. Employees are the most important audience in a layoff announcement, of course, and their feelings should be paramount in your planning. Not only do they have a personal stake in the news, but they also become unofficial messengers who relate and translate the information to the community. Whether they are told in a group meeting, in small sessions by their supervisors, or via a written bulletin, you should schedule your media activities so that most employees get the word about a half-hour before any reporter. If you are having your news release hand-carried to the media, a good rule of thumb is to let the messengers leave for the media's offices at the same time the news is released internally. That way you are sure the announcement actually is being made. If any employee gets to a phone to call a local reporter before your messenger has arrived, you can easily explain your announcement timetable and stress your organization's desire that your own employees hear the news first before any outsider. That kind of candor can only increase a journalist's impression of your planning skills and adherance to the delicate balance between the media's right to know and your employees' feelings.

On a related note, television assignment editors often call in a layoff situation to ask permission to go inside your plant or office to interview your employees on camera and get their reactions to the news. Or radio stations ask to tape interviews with your workers. Their intent is to go after the human side of the story. You may feel this type of request not only will disrupt operations within your facility but also will intrude unnecessarily on your employees' privacy. Indeed, many feel such "sad news" stories bring out the worst in electronic journalism. Commentator James Wolcott summarized many people's views of television news when he criticized one program because it "does not really believe in covering stories—it simply takes a swipe at them, like a bear pawing the water for fish."[24]

If you do not wish to grant requests to film within your facility, your best course of action is, as always, to simply tell the truth: "We feel that arranging interviews with people who have just been told they are going to be laid off is not a very considerate thing to do. However, I [or another spokesperson] will be happy to give you an on-camera interview and provide background footage [or slides] showing our operations." That kind of explanation and cooperation sometimes will satisfy TV stations—especially when you offer footage, since theirs is a moving and visual medium. Similarly, taping an interview with your CEO and offering it to a radio station as an actuality can result in good pick-up of your statement. However, broadcast journalists often will insist on on-site coverage outside your building, and you would do well to cooperate with this request. As well, with or without your permission some will assign their reporters to interview employees as they pour out of the gates or drive out of the parking lot. As long as the interviews are not taking place on the job and the reporter has no way of talking only with people actually laid off, you would do well to avoid narrow arguments over the location of the public property line. Better to stay in your office and let your employees decide for themselves if they want to be interviewed, because they now are on their own time. It is on occasions like this that companies and organizations discover how their workers really feel about them and how successful their internal communications programs have been. Some have been pleasantly surprised to hear their employees look right into the TV camera and say the company did everything it could, including offering voluntary time off and early retirement incentives, to avoid a layoff, but sagging sales left them no choice. Such unsolicited testimonials are priceless in positively influencing the local community's reaction to your news.

MAJOR ACCIDENTS AND OTHER CATASTROPHES

Handling media relations after an accident or during a crisis such as a product recall that runs on for several days or weeks will tax the talents of the most seasoned professional. Your ability to function well—to meet the needs of the media and the community for public information while not jeopardizing the personal and legal rights of employees and your organization—will depend on split-second decisions and uncommon judgment. Some organizations put their heads in the sand and pray an emergency will never develop. Savvy ones, on the other hand, devise strategies to deal with the worst eventuality. For the sake of both you and your employer, it is wise to develop a detailed written plan for dealing with catastrophes—and get it reviewed and blessed by upper management long before it is needed. Circulate the plan widely throughout your organization with a cover memo from your CEO summarizing its purpose and stressing its importance. Then review it annually to see if it needs updating.

Kansas City communicators learned first-hand the value of written crisis plans when two skywalks in the Hyatt Regency Hotel there crashed to the floor amid revelers at a weekly tea dance. The hotel disaster was the worst in the city's history, with 111 dead and 188 injured. Judy Hasse, public relations coordinator for St. Luke's Hospital, explained that a control center was quickly set up to handle the information needs of the public and the media. "We have a mass casualty plan, as do all hospitals," she said, "and specific guidelines for the communications staff are included. Our plan worked. It's terrible that it had to be used, but it worked." Possibly the most complex communications task fell to Crown Center Redevelopment Corporation, a wholly owned subsidiary of Hallmark Cards and owner of the Hyatt building. Hyatt Hotels, a division of Hyatt Corporation, operates and manages the Hyatt Regency under a management agreement. "The situation was unusual because there were so many entities involved," said Steve Doyal, public relations director for Crown Center. "Our first activity was to provide the media with clearance for photos and facts about the hotel. The next move was to attempt to organize information about the disaster. Our efforts during the week following the tragedy were focused on the investigation. We tried to provide as much information as possible. None of the crisis communications sessions I've been to could have prepared me for something of this magnitude, but it certainly helped to have a detailed plan to work from."[25]

Keeping the plan current also is a necessity. E. Zoe McCathrin, director of public relations for BancOhio National Bank in Columbus, says: "When a crisis occurs you need to move. It's too late to worry about putting together a plan of action." McCathrin speaks with the voice of experience, after living through more than 50 robberies, attempted robberies, and other crimes against various branches around Ohio. "In each case public relations professionals, armed with a step-by-step crisis plan, facilitated the flow of information from bank protection and law enforcement officials to the media, while protecting the identity of the victims," McCathrin said. The plan, developed in 1976 in response to increasing crimes of violence against the bank, is reviewed and updated regularly. "After each crisis situation the bank personnel involved meet to discuss what happened, and make suggestions for improving the procedure."[26]

As you develop a written crisis communications plan, a key point you will want to make clear to the top decision makers of your company or client is that the definition of a crisis—and thus of a legitimate news story—is a relative thing. In a small town, one person hospitalized as a result of an accident on a production line can generate more coverage in the local newspaper than a major earthquake in China because the community editor knows readers care about their neighbors. A few people picketing in front of your office over a work dress code can be big news—and front-page photograph and television footage material—even when you feel the issue is trivial in light of broader labor relations matters. Incidents like these do not require activation of a full-fledged crisis plan, but they do require attention to many of the same principles. Indeed, your prompt, matter-of-fact management of smaller incidents will go a long way toward containing them so they do not develop into major media events. You may even convince reporters the issue is so routine as to not be newsworthy.

The first step in a crisis communications plan is a detailed procedure for alerting whoever must know that a major accident or other critical event has taken place. As the person responsible for media relations, your name should be right at the top of the list— immediately after the CEO's and the police or fire department. There should be at least one back-up person for each of you. The guidelines should be written with a "when in doubt, call" tone. You want the night foreman or security guard to feel you would rather be informed about something that turns out to be minor— even if it involves a phone call in the middle of the night—than have an unexpected crisis explode in your face. There should be one or two people on this first-team call list who are experts in any field that might make crisis news—including legal, financial, personnel and technical expertise.

The second step is to establish who will be in charge of the disaster team and thus your source of information—and to get agreement on the fact that you or your staff will be the only source of information to the news media. This is the single most critical element of the plan. Only if you have a direct line to the place where all policy and corrective action decisions are being made can you function properly. Only if the media know who to contact can you expect accurate presentation on the facts and your organization's position. Immediate response to journalists' queries—often measured in minutes rather than hours—is critical in a crisis situation. You do not want to shoot from the hip. Nor do you want to be so deliberate that you approach paralysis and miss a reporter's deadline. As a corrolary, you need to designate back-ups for yourself and the head of the operations team in case the crisis demands 24-hour-a-day staffing. You should arrange for contact people at any remote location who would handle reporters on the scene under your direction or until you could get there.

After the initial contact list and the designations of who is in charge, other components of the crisis plan should include the following:

1. Determine an appropriate location in your headquarters or main office where you could set up an operations and news center if it were necessary. Make sure it has adequate telephone and data facilities, typewriters or word processors, telecopy and duplicating machines, news release paper, and other office supplies. Locate the nearest food sources and hotels or motels, and

arrange contingency credit and billing procedures—they may be necessary not only for your organization but also for the media.

2. List appropriate public officials, including the mayor, legislators, senators, union leaders, heads of local consumer groups, or other key opinion leaders whom you might want to keep informed on an ongoing basis depending on the nature and severity of the catastrophe. Include their office and home phone numbers. Initiating contact and opening up a communications channel in a crisis situation often can turn a potential protester into an ally.

3. Ensure the availability of a large supply of background information kits including photos and other basic materials about your organization. A crisis often is covered by spot news reporters who normally are not familiar with your business or industry.

4. Create a responsibilities list for your staff using a worst-case scenario. For example, if you decided to host an on-site news conference, who would arrange for transportation for the media? Handle the start-up? Write a news release? Get it duplicated? Update your background piece? Hire a photographer? Get pagers or mobile phone units? Brief your CEO or chief spokesperson? Arrange for technical experts who also can communicate in everyday language with reporters? Refresh their interview techniques skills? Control media access to the disaster site? Control statements issued by the hospital?

5. Find out where the nearest hospital, fire, police, poison control, ambulance, and other emergency services are for each of your facilities. Make that list available to the management and security people at each location—and a part of your written crisis communications plan.

6. Major catastrophes can affect the price of your company's stock. Make sure your plan includes an investor relations or financial analysts contact person you can alert if necessary. Consider advising your CEO to contact your board of directors or trustees so they hear the news from you rather than the news media.

7. Similarly, there may be a need for someone in your organization to contact regulatory agencies like the Food and Drug Administration, Occupational Safety and Health Administration, Securities and Exchange Commission, or a state or local commission. Many "bad news" situations have government implications. Also be prepared in case any information given to a government agency finds its way to the media.

8. Legal and insurance ramifications must be foremost in your mind during any significant crisis. Establish a legal liaison with whom you can have instantaneous access or minute-by-minute contact if you need it. Statements to the media should describe the nature of the crisis—but not speculate on its cause nor give a dollar estimate of damage.

9. Employees are a key constituency during any crisis. So are distributors, wholesalers, retailers, and suppliers. Establish separate communications channels for them or they will tie up phone lines into your news center that were intended for reporters' use. If they know the facts they are less likely to speculate or spread rumors. Make sure your labor relations people are involved in any decisions affecting union-represented employees.

10. If the crisis continues for several days, establish and stick to a briefing schedule. Your spokesperson, advisers, and the media all will be grateful for a respite from their vigil. Tired participants can result in indiscreet revelations, inaccurate quotes, and safety problems. Even when you do not know all the facts and answers, let the media know what you know on a continuing basis—before they find out from other sources.

11. Continually remind yourself and your spokesperson to be sensitive to the needs of their audiences as they discuss an accident or other disaster. Business people tend to be concerned with money, facts, figures, and the reality of a situation; reporters and their readers or viewers are normally more interested in the emotional, dramatic, human aspects of the case. Remember the adage "Soldiers fight for their country but die for their buddies." Both your attitude and your actions should show serious concern for your employees and the public—particularly if anyone has been injured or killed. It is not necessary to accept blame; in fact, for legal reasons you will want to avoid that. But your answer to the question "What are you going to do about it?" should clearly explain your corrective action in terms people will understand. Be succinct—especially if you are on radio or television. To those who say their story is too complicated to be told in 30 seconds, ABC-TV News economic correspondent Dan Cordtz has responded that corporations spend billions of dollars every year on commercials which are 30 seconds long—and presumably informative enough to be worth the expense.[27] It is not easy to boil your position down to a paragraph, but it can be done. It must be, if you want your point made on TV or radio.

12. If you are launching an investigation, it can be valuable to name outside experts who will be asked to give an independent evaluation. Your objective should be not merely to give information but also to generate support for the way your organization is handling the incident.

13. A decision to withhold negative news should be made only after you have considered the implications of the fact that subsequent revelations of your containment activities may generate more publicity than the news would have. Remember that the ubiquitous presence of copying machines and wide-ranging powers of legal subpoenas have almost made the private memo or report obsolete.

14. Conversely, do not overreact to a problem in one branch or area and assume it automatically is an issue elsewhere. Gather the facts and scope the problem before you act. If you alert offices all over the country without determining you have only an isolated incident, you could create news problems that never need arise.

ADVANTAGES OF APPROVED PLANS

There are many advantages to having an approved crisis communications plan in place for your organization long before an accident, fire, strike, product recall, or other disaster occurs. Obviously, such a plan limits the number of decisions that must be made in an emergency mode. It also legitimizes your role as a valued member of any crisis team. And it serves to remind others of the importance of long-term relations with the news media. On the tactical front it can also encourage participation in interview techniques training as a matter of course for anyone who might be involved in crisis communications. Businessmen and women know their subjects far better than any reporter who will ever interview them—but their performances during an accident or other catastrophe can make it appear they are ignorant or—worse—covering up something. When the emergency hits it is far too late to learn spokesperson skills and cultivate communication with the media.

Further, when you have set procedures in place you are prepared if you want to be the first to reveal negative news. There are many advantages of this course of action. You are more likely to get your story accurately reported by the media. You are less likely to be on the defensive. You may get credit for honestly admitting a mistake—and caring enough about your customers and the public to speak up and let them know about it. You will establish yourself as the source of information, a partnership position most reporters will think twice about before exploiting. Taking the initiative may avoid making a hero out of your attacker, be it an unhappy employee or a self-styled consumer advocate. You are also more likely to have the story covered for only one day and then forgotten. Your objective in handling bad news is to get it out of the way and prevent it from becoming a continuing news story. Forthrightly explaining the situation and emphasizing remedial action will usually accomplish this objective, since there will be little of the charges and countercharges between two sides that characterize ongoing news stories. Further, the Securities and Exchange Commission and major stock exchange regulations may require publicly held firms to disclose negative news if it could have a material effect on the financial status of your company or client and affect shareowners' investment decisions.

Recalling a defective product may be embarrassing and costly for a company. It also can make good business sense and protect both consumers and the corporate image from irreparable harm. For example, John J. Nevin, head of The Firestone Tire & Rubber Company, said in retrospect in 1981 that his company should have voluntarily recalled its infamous Firestone 500 tires long before the government insisted on the recall in 1978. Although it was concerned about the number of free replacements it was making, Nevin said Firestone should have initiated action before lengthy government hearings into the tire's safety tarnished the company image.[28] The candid approach worked well for Bank of America in 1980 when a customer complaint revealed that the bank's service charges on consumer loans were exceeding state limits. Bob Feinberg, the vice president who directs news relations for the bank, said: "We recommended to management that the bank take the initiative, announce the mistake along with the remedy of paying everybody back in full, and station spokespeople around our branch system to answer press questions. Some executives felt uncomfortable about this and thought the bank would look silly. We said we'd look sillier if we refunded $1000 to a reporter who would run the story and start an incident that would drag on for months. We announced the mistake and it was in and out of the papers in 48 hours."[29]

Johnson & Johnson adopted a similar strategy of openness with the news media after tampered capsules of cyanide-laced Extra Strength Tylenol caused seven deaths in Chicago in 1982. This was a departure from the company's previous media relations posture, although in fairness such a decision must have been easier to make because company officials knew the tragedy was not their fault. Media interest was immediate and intense. "We decided right away to answer every single press inquiry," said Lawrence G. Foster, vice president for communications. Over the weekend following the tragic poisonings, the company, which gets three or four calls from reporters on a normal day, answered nearly 300 media calls.[30] Chairman James Burke appeared on TV programs like "Donahue" and "60 Minutes." When the company decided to keep the Tylenol brand alive in a repackaged container, it hosted a massive news conference via a 30-city teleconferencing hook-up. Ironically, then, the media—which had unwittingly created a potential marketing disaster for Tylenol—became the vehicle for its comeback.

Johnson & Johnson said it received more than 125,000 press clippings on the tragedy, nearly all of them favorable. More importantly, Tylenol regained more than 80% of the market share it held before the poisonings, a feat one market analyst called "a miracle, pure and simple."[31] "Johnson & Johnson has effectively demonstrated how a major business ought to handle a disaster," wrote Jerry Knight in the *Washington Post*. "From the day the deaths were linked to the poisoned Tylenol until the recall ... J&J has succeeded in portraying itself to the public as a company willing to do what's right regardless of cost. Serving the public interest has simultaneously saved the company's reputation. That lesson in public responsibilities—and public relations—will survive at J&J regardless of what happens to Tylenol."[32]

Johnson & Johnson's Tylenol ordeal demonstrated the value of openness and consistency with the media when an organization finds itself involved in a major disaster. Such responsiveness does not always mean the end of the story, however. Sometimes publicity begets publicity. If a wire service picks up your news and transmits it to their member newspapers or stations, you could get calls from reporters across the country or on the other side of the world. Or the news could be carried by smaller papers and stations with limited staff exactly as received—the so-called rip and read style of journalism. This practice makes it critical in bad news situations that you have maintained a close working relationship with local bureau chiefs of wire services so that they are more likely to call you for comment and to verify stories before they are sent out over the wires. It also argues for you to make a practice of delivering your releases to wire services first. You may want to consider subscribing to Associated Press, United Press International, Dow-Jones or other wire services, depending on the nature of your business, so you can monitor and immediately correct any erroneous or misleading information that goes out on your organization. What they transmit over their wires in the first few minutes after news breaks has a significant impact on the way a story is covered in your area, throughout the nation, and sometimes even internationally. Thousands of publications or stations reaching millions of people get much of their news from wire services, so their influence should not be underestimated.

Perhaps all you can realistically hope for when you are involved in negative news is that the media get the facts right and portray your organization as being concerned and actively involved in fixing what went wrong. Including a positive and personable quote from your CEO high up in the news release or response statement, hand-carrying the story to the media, beating your opposition to the wire services so your statement is carried first, initiating phone contacts and offering to set up interviews for key reporters, answering media questions late into the night—all these tactics will go a long way toward ensuring fair coverage for your company or client. Clearly, honesty is always the best policy because reporters and the public will eventually learn that they have been fed half-truths or had information withheld. In the final analysis it will be the professional relationships you have established over the years with the news media—combined with the essential rightness of your organization's position—that will determine how reporters and editors handle your news.

Effective news media relations is much like effective selling— it takes time to position yourself in journalists' minds as a necessary and credible resource over the long term, and to build relationships when new reporters come on the scene. Because they control the main channels for the rapid dissemination of information in a bad news situation, reporters' attitudes are of paramount importance to you. Their misunderstanding or hostility could garble—or perhaps completely change—your message before it reaches their readers or viewers, who are your customers, employees, volunteers, and shareowners. Whether or not they have a legal right to such information, these stakeholders are demanding to know how organizations that affect their lives socially and economically conduct their affairs—particularly when something goes wrong. The true test of your media relations skills, your top management's confidence in you and, ultimately, your organization's standing in the community will come in a negative situation. Indeed, it will be your record of accuracy, honesty and plain speaking that will give you credibility and carry your company or client successfully through the emergency.

9

MEASUREMENT

How to Evaluate and Justify
your Program

In the United States alone, there are more than 1700 daily newspapers, 700 Sunday papers, 8200 weekly papers, and 6200 trade and consumer magazines. Add to this hundreds of television and radio stations and you can begin to see the scope of a media relations program.

While it probably is not the intent of your particular media relations program to reach all of these media outlets, it should be your intent to know, insofar as possible, how many of your targeted media used your release, commented on your problem, or applauded your organization's efforts through editorials.

Measurement of the various relations activities is generally the forgotten element of the program. In fact, one current handbook on publicity does not even include a section on measurement. When measurement is mentioned, it is often as a knee-jerk reaction to the question "How did we do on that notice about the new parking lot?" But, measurement should be as well thought out, as well planned, and as well executed as the rest of your media relations program.

You should know if you want to measure:

1. The relationship you have with the media representatives

2. The impact your messages have on the publics you wish to reach (do they act the way you want them to?)
3. The numbers of people you reach via the media
4. The way your message is perceived by the public (do they feel about you the way you want them to?)
5. How many media use your message
6. All of the above and more

METHODS

No matter how large or small your operation may be, every well-run media shop should have some method for monitoring and evaluating the results of its output.

Measurement of press activities used to be easily recorded by counting the number of column inches in the daily newspaper and the number of newspapers which used the release. That was sufficient unto the day—the day before fragmentation of audiences, electronic media, and satellite transmissions.

Changes in the media field itself as well as increased sophistication in measurement techniques have brought about changes in the way we measure our work.

Do-It-Yourself

If your media relations activities are centered in a small geographic area, a city, county, or state, for instance, you may want to consider creating your own monitoring/clipping arrangement for both print and electronic media.

For the print side, this means you begin by subscribing to all the publications that receive your news releases or are likely to cover your industry or organization. These publications could run the gamut from business and financial publications to detailed engineering journals, trade newsletters, and industry-specific magazines.

Assign one person responsibility for reading the publications. This person, the reader, will become familiar with the style and arrangement of each of the publications and will not have to waste valuable time wading through sections that would not carry your type of news.

The reader also will be in a position to notice if certain

publications are changing in their style of coverage, if they increase (or decrease) coverage of your company, and other trends.

Reading should not be given as an extra assignment to a staff person who already has a full work load. Reading should be a primary responsibility, if at all possible. This assures that the reading is done in a timely manner and that subsequent results—with their ramifications—are on your desk as soon as possible.

The reader should cut or copy each article that pertains to your organization or subject matter and attach the article to bond paper. At the top of the sheet should go the name of the publication, the date of publication, and the page number.

Television and radio monitoring can be as simple or as complex as you desire.

The best method of the do-it-yourself variety perhaps is to assign people within your organization to watch specific television stations in your area and/or listen to radio newscasts.

Television has few lengthy news programs and they generally fall into three time slots: morning, evening, and late evening. Although there are numerous news breaks and news updates throughout the day, your interest probably will be in whether your organization appears during one of the lengthier, prime-time shows.

Radio, on the other hand, has newscasts quite often. They can be every half hour, every hour, or even constantly (witness the advent of all-news radio stations). There are, however, two prime times which may be of interest to you: morning and afternoon commuting times when decision makers, thought leaders, and overall business audiences are driving to and from work.

For both television and radio, the viewer/listener has a relatively simple task of noting the name of the station (call letters as well as popular name), the name of the program, and the time of day the item was mentioned. A one-line summary of the content also is useful, such as: "Repeated announcement of new company president" or "Used announcement, mispronounced president's name" or "Information was correct, used film footage of manufacturing facility".

Clipping/Monitoring Services

If your activities are far-reaching or complex, from a regional effort to a nationwide or even international campaign, you may find it advantageous to use clipping and/or monitoring services. What you gain in convenience and peace of mind, however, you might lose in money, as clipping services can become quite expensive.

The best way to make sure you are getting full value is to clearly define, both within your organization and with the service, what it is you want monitored or clipped. By starting out with a well-thought-out program, you stand less chance of being disappointed later.

For example, you may want only those clips which carry the name of your organization, such as the American Heart Association. Or, you may want to have clips which also talk generically of your product or service offering, such as heart disease information or heart transplants. There also might be variations of your organization's name which should be noted by the clipping agency.

If your organization is considering launching a media relations or public relations campaign, you may wish to monitor other organization's activities to help give you an idea of how your campaign *might* be received.

For instance, if your company is going to introduce a new method of installing solar heating units, you might want to see what the media is saying already about solar heat generally and installation of heating units specifically. You might want to determine the media's understanding of solar heating or the types of artwork or photography most often used.

Similarly, you might want to be aware of the public's attitude about care of the elderly before introducing a new senior citizen program.

As you can see, a clipping/monitoring service can be as finite or as general as you direct. Certainly, such a service can be more thorough than you or your staff members because it has people who are professionally trained to monitor and clip.

These clipping/monitoring agencies vary in pricing methods. Some may charge a flat fee for a specified number of print clips; others may charge a monthly reading rate plus a cost per clip. The important thing here is to check costs ahead of time and try to anticipate which system will be better for your organization.

Many of the monitoring agencies now offer electronic clips as well. They record both radio and television newscasts on a local, regional, or even national level, sort through the newscasts on playback, and listen for clients' names or subject areas.

Electronic clips can be offered to the client in two ways: a copy of the audio- or videotape, or a transcript of the segment of the program pertaining to the client. Either way can be quite expensive if you are in the media extensively. You should carefully think out the possible uses for such electronic clips before engaging in securing them. For instance, do you really need six variations of the same product announcement? Or ten radio spots naming your new president? What use do you have for the electronic clips? These clips take up shelf space quickly and can devour a budget rapidly.

One advantage in using a clipping agency is that the service will provide up-to-date circulation or viewing/listening audience figures. A return of only one clip on your news release might not seem too successful until you are able to note that the item was used on network nightly news or in the morning paper with a one million circulation.

WHAT TO DO WITH CLIPS

Many media relations offices look like the last vestiges of a pack rat convention. Clips, newspapers, magazines, and tear sheets freely decorate the confines.

The problem seems to be that few people know what to do with all the clips after they come in. There are several solutions to this dilemma, all of which clearly point to one thing: document your successes and failures and let others in your organization know what is happening.

The simplest method of this is to organize your clips, from the daily reading in your office and/or your clipping service, make copies of those articles and then present the copies to the key executives who need to be aware, on a daily basis, of news about the company and/or field of interest.

A variation of this procedure is to take the clipped articles and write a synopsis of each. The final piece, which should be no more than one or two pages, is reproduced each day, again for circulation to executives.

Either method performs a highly needed service for your key officers. They do not have the time to peruse all the publications that deal with your industry or service area. They look to you to perform that service. The clips or synopses do not have to be specifically about your organization, but they should be relevant to the business.

A more detailed presentation of clips should include an analysis. For example, if you have had to announce the closing of a manufacturing location which employed 1000 people, you probably are anxious to know how the media dealt with that story. Did they treat it objectively? Were the editorials damaging or supporting? Were the explanations of the closing repeated accurately? Was there additional pick-up on the wire services?

By gathering all of the clips, both print and electronic, and answering these types of questions, you can identify certain traits about the media, reporters, and newscasters.

You might notice that one reporter seemed to consistently misunderstand, and thus, misrepresent, the story behind the closing while all others got the story correct. You might also notice that all the headlines or television leads were straightforward and not of the "scare" variety.

This information tells you that you—and the executives who helped you—put together material that was easily understood. It tells you that the media have an understanding of the situation and that your story was handled fairly with only the one exception. You cannot ask for much more than that; the one reporter should be invited in for a briefing on the business because clearly, he or she misunderstood. And the people who assisted you should be given a pat on the back for their efforts.

This type of analysis ideally should be done with each major news event. It also can be done over an extended period of time with an ongoing, low-key campaign.

Such a campaign might be created to increase public awareness of the many ramifications of drunk driving. Articles supporting this theme would be placed with general and trade media over a long period of time—a minimum of a year although two to three years would be better. Remember: just as in advertisements, the public only begins to retain a message after hearing or seeing it several times.

Clips of the articles would be gathered and kept. Periodic reports could be prepared showing how many articles have appeared; how many people read those articles; which geographic regions use the articles the most; what type of headlines appear;

what types of audiences are reading the material; if the articles are completely rewritten or used almost in the original form; how many additional articles were created by the media based on information that was sent out.

The nice thing about a long-term project such as this one is that the program can be changed along the way to counter any negative items which might be appearing. For example, if the articles are being totally rewritten, then you need to look again at your releases and find out why. Are they not in the proper journalistic style? Are they full of typos? Did you fail to put on your contact name and number?

Also, if articles are not being run in certain publications, find out why. Do they not fit the style of the publication? Are they going to the wrong editor? Are they missing the deadlines?

The final report on a long-term project should talk about both the positives and negatives. It should tell what was accomplished by the campaign and explain both how the external audience benefitted from it and what the internal media relations staff learned from it.

Clips also can be used to spot trends in your industry or service area. If coverage of your organization changes, perhaps it is because of new activities in Washington from environmentalists or labor lobbyists. Perhaps something else has occurred to make reporters and editors look anew at your company, industry, or organization.

Where to keep clips—if you keep them at all—can sometimes be a problem. If you have announced the opening of a new office or manufacturing facility, then all the clips of that announcement clearly should go with the archives. But what of the others?

A clever way to distribute clips is to look for people in the organization who might have an interest in the story. Attorneys, for example, often need clips that mention your company or association in regard to a particular activity, such as pending litigation, resolved litigation, or just in reference to a general topic, such as safe manufacturing procedures.

Attorneys also will be interested in clips that show possible trends which might affect them: increasing numbers of age discrimination suits, possible ramifications of transborder data flow, or Good Samaritan laws.

Clips mentioning employees should be sent to those employees as a courtesy service from the media relations group. Even if an employee bowls a 300 game in another league and it somehow shows up in your clips, send it to the employee with a congratulatory note. If one of your executives gives a speech to a local civic organization and it is written up, he or she would appreciate having the clips. When you send out a news release announcing a new executive, keep track of the resulting coverage for your own analysis, but also send copies of the clips to the executive. The subject-matter experts you use as spokespersons for interviews also would appreciate clips on their topics as well as copies of the articles in which they appeared. Clips on products can go to the appropriate product manager or market manager. Clips talking about what a good corporate citizen your company is should be shared with as many people as possible.

As part of your regular media relations reporting and measuring, you should occasionally note how much money your organization would have had to spend in paid advertisements for the same amount of editorial space or air time you managed to get for the organization. This is not intended to detract from advertising; instead, it shores up the power of positive media relations.

MEASURING THE VAGUE

Measuring how people react to a media relations campaign is something best left to public opinion experts and pollsters. There are times when this knowledge will be essential for strategic planning and so it will be worth the time and money invested.

Quite simply, all you are trying to find out is whether or not the public acted in a way you wanted them to because of your media program. It could be that one of the objectives of your campaign to increase public awareness of the ramifications of drunk driving was to get the public to write their congressional representatives for new legislation. To get that kind of knowledge would require the assistance of professional public opinion gatherers.

On a less exact level, you might just need to know how many people attended the open house of your new facility or the festival in the park as a result of your media efforts.

Determining how people *feel* about your organization also is something that can be done professionally. There are ways to find out if your print and electronic clips are viewed as positive, neutral, or negative. Although you might be able to guess at such responses based on key verbs and adjectives in the articles, it still is best to have an objective, outside firm perform this service for you. Such information is excellent to have during critical times in your organization's life; for example, during labor negotiations or a major catastrophe. The objective is to see if the message you are sending is received as a positive or neutral message. If the message is perceived as negative, you can at best hope to pull it up to neutral. The important item to note is that you *can* measure beyond the number of column inches and numbers of clips—and determine impact as well as mechanics.

Combining all these measurements together for a long-term campaign can produce astonishing results. Still using the drunk driving campaign as an example, we can find out:

1. How many people are reading/hearing the desired message
2. In what geographic areas these people reside
3. Which media are using the message
4. If the public is acting upon our message in the way we want them to
5. If the public views our message in a positive, neutral, or negative manner
6. If we have done better in the last three months than the three months previous

Correlations can then be drawn between the number of drunk driving incidents in a certain geographic area before, during, and after the media campaign. If the results are positive, you can share in the credit. If the results are negative, find out why and begin a new campaign.

Unless you are dealing with only a few media, you will probably want to consider a media relations audit every so often. For objectivity, the audit should be done for you, rather than by you.

The media relations audit works like this: an opinion research firm surveys editors and news directors in the region you specify. They ask such questions as how responsive an organization is to media inquiries, whether the editor knows who to contact for information at an organization, the quality of the news releases received, and the courtesy of the organization in dealing with the media.

The questionnaire can be structured to deal with any aspect of news media relations you want it to. Generally, the survey asks about several companies simultaneously to avoid the "halo syndrome" where the editor might say good things about your organization because you are asking and you are a friend. Having several companies participate also cuts down on the costs.

Unless you know your way around polling techniques and statistical analysis, you probably should not conduct such an audit yourself.

This type of audit actually measures the *relationship* you have with the media representatives. So, when the audit comes back saying you have some journalists out there who do not think you are doing a very good job, you know you have to start from square one to build up a better relationship.

An audit also will help you continue to meet the needs of the media, which should be one of your primary functions. An audit can be expensive but it is well worth the effort if your media relations program is extensive and if you have several people in your shop and want to make sure they all have good relationships with the media on their beat.

No matter what the extent of your media operations, you should have built-in measurement techniques. After all, you have put a lot of work into creating a program that will tell your organization's story to the public. Surely you want to measure the impact of that story and relate how that helps your organization meet its goals and objectives. To do any less than that would be to do less than the best professional work you can do.

10

THE FUTURE

Expanding your Counselor Role

The evolution is so natural and so subtle that you may not be aware of the metamorphosis until it has occurred. One day you are responding to a journalist's question on why your organization has a certain policy. While your lips are providing the answer, your mind is asking, "Why indeed?" Or you might be briefing a spokesperson for your organization before a major media interview, when suddenly it becomes obvious to both of you that a practice is woefully out of date. So together you work out a plan to change it. Or you are writing the opening remarks for your CEO to deliver at a news conference when you cross over the line from simply articulating organizational policy to actually framing it. Your role has changed. Your responsibilities expand. Like a stained-glass window that diffuses light as it passes through, enhancing it by the addition of a myriad of beautiful colors, you find yourself contributing to your organization's policies and helping to shape its future. You have become an entrepreneur in the broadest sense whether or not you run your own company, because you are truly breaking new ground. You have become a public relations counselor.

When President Kennedy asked Edward R. Murrow to

become director of the U.S. Information Agency, Murrow reportedly responded that he would be happy to do so "provided it is understood that I shall be in on the takeoffs as well as the crash landings."[1] That is a position we all argue for—albeit perhaps not so cleverly. Too often the task of media relations people is to make the rough *appear* smooth, rather than to carefully apply sandpaper to make that objective a reality. In Chapter 8, for example, we discussed ways your expertise could offer temporary relief from the symptoms in crisis situations. In this chapter we will address ways you can help cure the disease.

The access that our media relations responsibilities gives us—not only to top management but also to the decision-making processes of our company or client—brings with it a great obligation. We can take apparently random sequences of events and help translate them into an actionable agenda. We can ensure our organization's decision makers have access to public opinion and attitudes so they can evaluate their actions against perception as much as reality. After all, every misconception begins with a certain element of truth. Much like products, public issues too have life cycles. We can help identify emerging issues early enough so our organizations can shape and manage rather than just respond to them. Counseling is much more than merely offering advice. It is acting as a sort of strategic glue, bringing together input from all available external and internal sources to ensure a catholic rather than a parochial view. It is selectively sorting information and focusing only on events that are important and contribute to understanding. A good counselor will relate and interpret the facts; a great one will understand and enhance the meaning.

"You should try to get yourself positioned as one who has a special sensing system and thus can anticipate problems in time to solve them before they erupt publicly," advises Harold W. Burlingame, Vice President–External Affairs at AT&T Information Systems. "Public relations people need to be an integral part of the planning process if you are to help your organization anticipate and prepare for change. To be credible, however, you have to demonstrate a solid understanding of the business and appreciation for its operations problems. Without that knowledge you will have great difficulty being accepted as an equal member of the management team."

Inevitably there will be those who continue to slot their line and staff people into different categories, tolerating discussion of emerging issues only in the ivory-tower offices of staff people, and insisting that concerns such as budgets, production timetables and inventory control dominate the time of operations managers. These executives must have forgotten the lessons learned by General Motors, which watched helplessly as the power of Ralph Nader and his consumer movement grew strong enough to kill the Corvair. Or they choose to ignore the experience of nonprofit associations and arts groups which ceased to exist in the early 1980s after government grants dried up because they had not previously developed community loyalty and deep financial ties with their constituents. Yet a growing number of companies formally tie issues monitoring to their corporate planning systems or include issues management in their performance appraisal systems. These include General Electric, Norton-Simon, Bank of America, General Mills, Ciba-Geigy, Connecticut General, Union Carbide, AT&T, International Paper, Eaton Corporation, Allied Chemical, and the Standard Oil Companies of California and Indiana.[2]

Almost all the critical problems facing your organization today and in the future are public relations problems in the broadest sense of the term. Like Rubik's cube, the solutions can be deceptively simple in appearance. But not for long can the cosmetic touches of a publicity program obscure deeper blemishes in organizational policy or practice. You can help your top management look at each problem strategically, searching for ways well-thought-out actions can contribute to their permanent resolution. You can apply a touch of healthy skepticism since, as Carl Sagan put it: "Skeptical scrutiny is the means ... by which deep insights can be winnowed from deep nonsense."[3] You can reflect shareowner sentiment, customer concerns and employee expectations, for you are their voice within your organization just as you are its ears and eyes in the community and the marketplace. Instead of expending energies criticizing the media for inaccurate reporting, you can help your top management address the policies and practices that prompt investigative journalism and negative news stories. You have an opportunity to use the unique window you have to public opinion—those constant contacts with the news media—to act as an early warning system to the decision makers of your organizations: to perceive not only what is going on around you but also what is coming. You can become a catalyst for change. Like truffle hounds, dogs used in France to root out delicacies from the underground, you can search for signs of emerging concerns so your organization has a head start in addressing those that merit attention. The length and breadth of the list may be awesome. Isolating and defining the underlying causes may be difficult, much like grappling with Jell-O. To be effective, solutions must reflect an objective analysis of the problem, rather than merely respond to the needs of your company or client.

CURRENT ISSUES TO WATCH

Throughout this book we have given specific examples of what you need to be aware of in your capacity as a media relations professional. Here we offer but a selection of the issues you should be aware of as you move into the capacity of counselor. These are issues facing many organizations, depending on their type and way they do business.

Changes in Job Requirements

Unemployment resulting from the recession of the early 1980s tended to mask a fundamental change in the job market of most industrial nations. Opportunities in the manufacturing sector are both shrinking and changing. Meanwhile, new jobs are surfacing in the service and high-technology industries—jobs requiring skills that many employees simply do not possess. The semiskilled industrial worker, previously the backbone of smokestack industries such as auto, rubber and steel, is becoming an expensive burden as technological advances (e.g., robots) reduce the number of employees needed to produce goods and services. Equally profound changes are coming to the service and clerical sectors. Twenty-four-hour electronic terminals have replaced bank tellers, and at-home video shopping is beginning to supplant retail clerks. Computers have taken over not only arithmetic previously performed by low-level clerks, but also design work that formerly was the province of graphic artists and engineers. Technology will, of course, create new jobs and economic booms. For example, the industrialization of the American South was, to a great extent, a result of the invention of air-conditioning. But the critical issue of the social responsibilities and costs of applying new technology has been raised. Retraining workers is likely to become as high a priority as retooling machinery. Legislation requiring several months notice to employees and the community of plans to close a plant or other major facility that will result in heavy job losses is being introduced in many areas.

Employers can reduce unemployment tax costs in some areas—and buy public goodwill—by aggressively helping to place their laid-off workers in other jobs. Addressing and communicating such profoundly personal issues may be our most difficult challenge in the next decade.

Declining Promotion Opportunities

As a result of the baby boom of the late 1940s and early 1950s, a large number of workers—most of whom are better educated than their predecessors and approach their work differently—are impatient to move up the organizational ladder. On the opposite end of the spectrum, inflation and the trends toward raising or eliminating the retirement age and postponing payment of Social Security benefits have resulted in older workers holding on to their jobs. The result is a serious conflict of interests: Women, minorities and younger workers want more and better jobs, but older employees are not leaving their posts and creating openings. As a result, promotional possibilities seem to be more limited, and the gap between what people want at work and what is available is widening. To avoid layoffs and create movement, organizations are designing special incentive programs that encourage early retirement. The trick is to avoid losing too many good people or violating age discrimination laws. Again, intensely sensitive and personal concerns are involved.

Quality of Work Life

Organizations must also learn to manage "the new worker"— employees of the 1980s and 1990s who think of themselves as individuals first and employees second. They bring their own special talents and skills into the workplace, but they also bring a deep concern for how they are treated. Beyond fair play, employees of the 1980s—regardless of their ages—seek simple trust. They want to be respected enough to be counted on to do right—on their own. They want to put their personal imprint on their work, actively participate in decisions shaping the content of their jobs, and have a significant say in the standards that measure their contributions. "Quality of Work Life" programs—commonly known as QWL—refer to systematic efforts to involve employees in designing and carrying out improvements in their work conditions. They cover a wide range of areas from different measurement methods to job-sharing proposals. While employees seek more responsibility and involvement in business decisions affecting their lives, their employers are pursuing a different goal: improved productivity and service. The two objectives are not mutually exclusive. Organizations pioneering in QWL have discovered that involving workers in day-to-day decision-making has led to improvements in productivity, service, and employee morale. QWL—sensitively and honestly implemented—can become an organization's competitive edge.

Security of Computer Files

The widespread use of computers, word processors and other data processing terminals has made it simpler for businesses and associations to process information rapidly and accurately. They have also made it easier for people to make massive mistakes and to steal information. Ensuring the integrity of computer files is a fast-growing priority in many organizations. From inadvertent miscalculations of interest due bank customers to deliberate intrusions into a file to steal or destroy valuable business information, the losses—in terms of dollars and public confidence—can be great. New insurance policies are being created to cover damage to information as well as property. A growing segment of this new market is malpractice insurance for companies that write software to tell a computer how to perform a particular task. Such insurance is increasingly necessary as computers are used in such life-saving efforts as neurological diagnosis. Off-site storage of back-up computer tapes containing inventory and customer data, and reciprocal agreements between companies to process the tapes in case of a fire, major power failure or other disasters, also increasingly are being included in computer security plans.

Employee and Customer Privacy

With so much personal information stored in computers and other files, protecting the privacy of employee and customer information is becoming a volatile issue. Electronic safeguards built into the computer system and its software programs are valuable. But the collection and retention of unnecesssary, out of date, and, in some cases, illegal information is what draws a great deal of the concern and attention of consumer groups, legislators and the media. Where we buy our clothes, what restaurants we patronize, how many miles we drive in our cars, who we phone, how much insurance we carry, which hotels we stay in when we travel, how large are our mortgage payments—such routine yet intensely private information is available in electronic memories when we pay our bills by credit card or check.

Purging non-essential data and severely restricting access to computer files is being legislated where it is not voluntarily accepted as good business practice. The first signal of this trend was passage of the Fair Credit Reporting Act of 1970, a model not only because it was the first major U.S. legislation relating to privacy, but also because it granted the individual the right to know what is on file and to disclaim or dispute the information. Subsequent legislation and the Privacy Protection Study Commission established by the Privacy Act of 1974 attest to the importance of this very personal issue.

Protectionism and Other Trade Restrictions

The recessionary economy of the early 1980s and increasing world competition created new demands for curbs on imports of products and exports of technology as each country strived to save jobs for its citizens. The General Agreement on Tariffs and Trade, the main international accord setting trade rules, is seen by some as either unworkable or unenforceable. [4] In the United States much of the protectionism sentiment is directed at Japan, as that country's products take an increasing share in the auto, electronics and other key markets. Some governments subsidize their companies' competition in global markets with low-cost loans. In many basic industries, on the other hand, American and Canadian workers' high wages have priced their companies out of world markets.

Advances in information networks and transportation systems now allow businesses to set up offshore operations where employees do a variety of tasks from word processing to components manufacturing more cheaply than their North American counterparts. In retaliation there is a growing movement that calls for a variety of restrictions on foreign competitors or use of overseas workers, requirements for specific percentages of American or Canadian parts and labor in any goods sold in those countries, or aid to workers who lose their jobs because of imports. In the United States several state legislatures are considering procurement preference bills that would give a 5% to 10% advantage to firms whose primary place of business is in that state. Others object to such restrictions, arguing that healthy competition and the free flow of goods and technology encourage a growing worldwide economy and exchange of scientific ideas.

Deregulation and New Information Demands

The trend toward deregulation in the airline, trucking, banking and communications industries may indicate the public is becoming more pro-free enterprise in the 1980s. Although consumers may clamor less loudly for protection from the ills of the marketplace via government regulatory agencies than they did in the 1970s, today's self-reliant consumer is demanding more in the way of information as the best protection. There is growing criticism of business for its perceived philosophy of planned obsolesence and for not caring enough about quality and safety.[5] Consumer advocate groups are taking on spokesperson responsibilities for these issues, and the universality of their appeal almost guarantees wide publicity. This trend suggests the critical importance of a timely, credible and complete customer information program through a variety of channels, including the news media.

AN INTEGRAL PART OF THE CORPORATE PLAN

AT&T Technologies Vice Chairman Donald E. Procknow no doubt had in mind a complex and varied group of issues when he said: "Public relations people should not be used simply to write announcements of what we have decided—or, worse yet, to fancy up words someone else has written. We all benefit when public relations is brought in much earlier in the decision-making process. Public relations is a management tool just like any other in the company—a very, very important resource."[6] And Kenneth S. Jamron, president of Deaconness Hospital in Milwaukee, Wisconsin, expanded on that thought: "I believe communications is such an important function that it cannot be filtered through anyone else. It has to have the highest level and sit in on management decisions."[7]

Charles Marshall, chief executive officer of AT&T Information Systems, calls his public relations staff "not only the business' communicators, but the business' consciences as well." Paraphrasing the poet Robert Burns, he says we must help our organizations see ourselves as others see us to ensure top management is not insulated—even when hearing the public's or employees' views is painful. Further, he reminds us: "We cannot just react. We must be proactive. Your role is to determine how we want our various publics to view us, and then help us develop a game plan to make it happen. After all, you cannot make us look any better than we deserve to look."[8] Marshall articulates a view held by an increasing number of CEOs who have given their public relations people a status in the corporate and nonprofit worlds comparable to production, marketing, legal and finance staffs because their skills are recognized as vital to setting sophisticated strategies and meeting ambitious objectives.

An example of a direct contribution to the development of an organization's business practices by media relations professionals took place at the Teletype Corporation in Illinois. Further, the public relations and marketing people not only began working more closely together but also were integrated into the company's overall corporate business plan.

When John J. Pappas was named president of the corporation in early 1981, Teletype had been in existence for almost 75 years and a part of AT&T for 50 years. The company employs about 5000 people who design, manufacture, and market data communications products. Headquartered in Skokie, Illinois, Teletype has manufacturing facilities there as well as in Little Rock, Arkansas. In addition, it has a nationwide distribution and service organization. But it suffered from being a subsidiary of a subsidiary. Owned by Western Electric, which in turn was owned by AT&T, Teletype rarely was considered news by the national business and trade press. Like Cinderella, Teletype people often stayed home and tended house while sister companies garnered the publicity by going to the ball.

With the line between data communications and data processing blurring, and regulatory restrictions on AT&T's lines of business soon to be lifted, Western Electric knew that Teletype would play a key role in its future. One sign of the company's new prominence was Pappas' appointment—it was the first time Teletype had been headed by a full executive officer from the parent company. Accompanying that move was the development of an active media relations plan. Its objective was wider coverage of Teletype in the national business and trade press; its strategy was to use the appointment of Pappas and the publication of the company's first public annual report to issue news releases and initiate contacts with key reporters. National business and trade press reporters who cover the telecommunications industry are veteran AT&T watchers, ever alert to reading between the lines for indications of a change in corporate strategy. No effort had been made to promote Teletype as a separate entity before. Astute reporters read the signals and asked why. Coverage resulted in such publications as the *Wall Street Journal, New York Times, Electronic News, Telephony, Datamation,* and *Telecommunications Reports.*

From a strict media relations viewpoint, then, the plan was a success. But it was becoming increasingly clear that Teletype's media relations, sales promotions and employee communications people needed to better coordinate their efforts. As is the case in too many organizations, public relations and marketing were separated philosophically as well as organizationally. Each operated independently, rarely sharing plans or exposing their materials to each other's audience. They did not have management's blessing of their information plans, so they had no assurance their activities were supporting the corporate plan. Media relations responsibilities were split—sales promotions handled the trade press and public relations handled the local media.

Pappas created a six-person task force composed of media relations, marketing and public relations people to analyze Teletype's communications and promotions efforts and come up with recommendations for the corporation. Stressing that their charter was broad, he told task force members at their first meeting: "The areas you should consider are unlimited. I am not prejudging your work, except that I know the situation we are in today needs to be fixed. There are too many people in too many organizations working separately on various public relations and promotions efforts. I have no doubt each of those people is working in the interests of the corporation. But there is no way those separate efforts can present a unified picture of Teletype. Your task is to bring those tangents together—to ensure that we have an orchestrated, integrated promotions effort."[9]

It was an assignment based on public relations considerations, to be sure: Its first three objectives were to present a consistent image of Teletype in all media, and to all target audiences, internally and externally; to ensure everyone involved in producing media for Teletype understood the company's corporate objectives and had written, detailed, tactical plans to help achieve them; and to upgrade the professionalism of promotions and communications materials where necessary. The task furthermore was rooted in the economic imperatives facing all organizations in these times of scarce and expensive resources. Its fourth objective was to make more efficient use of the people, time and dollar resources devoted to promotions and communications by expanding distribution of selected materials. Its overall goal was firmly focused on helping to achieve the corporate mission: To increase sales and to position Teletype as a high-technology market leader in the design and manufacture of data products and systems.

As is true with so many significant projects, the more the task force investigated the more they found there was to learn. It is also true that many problems any organization has with its promotions efforts are caused by communicators getting incomplete direction—and being all too ready to accept it and rush into print with a news release, employee newspaper, sales brochure or advertisement. The task force knew that to be successful they had to put their greatest effort into the first steps where it would have been easy to cut corners—into detailed analysis of the organization's business plans and marketing strategies, into prioritization of target audiences, into a candid and often ego-shattering assessment of current promotional and communication efforts, and into thoughtful, realistic strategies based on how their talents could be used to help the organization meet its objectives.

After 2 months of investigation and analysis, the task force recommended 16 promotions and communications strategies that offered a coordinated, unified approach to planning, producing, and distributing Teletype's wide variety of promotional materials —whether they were traditionally perceived as public relations, advertising or marketing media. Included was a new definition of Teletype's current and future business—in effect, a new mission statement—based on interviews with its top executives. The strengths that the company brought to that mission also were documented, later to be translated by its advertising agency into a broad advertising campaign with the theme "Value sets us apart." Media relations activities were expanded and targeted news release lists developed. Public relations and marketing responsibilities were delineated so the skills of both were allied to offer more specialized service to the media and better results to the company.

Internal materials got equal emphasis, since it was important that employees perceive Teletype as a first-class company if customers were to have that opinion. In reality there is no such thing as an internal communications vehicle *per se*. Even when employee newspapers are distributed at work, they often are taken home where they become in effect another external communications vehicle—to employees' families and their friends, some of whom might well be customers or reporters. Employee media earn readership or viewership by the attractiveness of their appearance and the relevance of their content. The strategies included a redesign of various employee publications to give them a first-class, modern appearance—with a unified look so it was obvious they all came from the same company. Their editorial content received similar attention—they increased the number of interpretive pieces giving the "why" behind corporate actions, and decreased stories on sports activities and photographs of upper management doing nothing more than shaking hands and giving out awards (known in the trade as "grip and grin" pictures). Upgraded in appearance as well as content, these publications now can be sent to reporters and other key publics, thus achieving wider coverage for virtually no additional cost. To complete the information-sharing loop, new ads, major news media coverage and trade show participation became topics for the internal publications, so employees were aware of how their company's sales and corporate messages were being communicated to customers.

With its public relations and marketing functions organized to exploit each discipline's skills while at the same time pooling knowledge, Teletype was able to take full advantage of the visit to its headquarters in the fall of 1981 of New York and Chicago security analysts, investment advisors and portfolio managers. Pappas' keynote address became the basis of a news release that was picked up by the local and trade press. The media relations people in Little Rock got coverage in both local papers on their president's visit to the Arkansas plant to give the security analysts' presentation to his employees there. Reprinted in booklet form, Pappas' speech was distributed to employees, reporters, key customers and security analysts around the country.

PART OF THE MARKETING MIX

Clearly, marketing and media relations people must combine their talents to effectively meet their own objectives as well as contribute to the organization's overall goals. Communications and promotions are an important part of the marketing mix. They must support the marketing plan and be measured against its objectives. The appearance and content of internal and external media are significant not as ends in themselves but because they are a deliberate, integrated part of the overall marketing effort. No less than a sales brochure, every news release must have a specific purpose, be directed to a specific audience, and be part of an overall plan. Releases must be managed like any other part of the business. And they must support the organization's sales and marketing objectives. It is a challenging approach that assumes top-to-bottom understanding of where the organization is going and how it plans to get there. It is a long-term project—influencing opinions takes time, and some results are hard to quantify.

The Teletype case illustrates corporate America's growing belief that media relations and other communications skills can play an important role in promoting sales—and in contributing to business policy before it is made. That recognition has elevated these functions both literally and figuratively within most organizations to the point where they now are valued participants in top-level councils. As Pappas put it: "You show me a market-driven organization and I'll show you a place where public relations considerations are an integral part of the planning process. CEOs should take advantage of all the expertise they can gather before they make decisions. Public relations is a valuable management resource. And media relations specialists in particular can offer insight into the shifting demands of the marketplace as a result of their contacts with reporters, who often reflect our customers' opinions."

The right to offer candid counsel and expect confidence in our advice does not flow automatically from our role as the media relations spokesperson, however. It must be earned. We must do as good a job of preparing a case to persuade our management, board or other decision makers as we do when we are preparing a case to persuade the public. We can take a lesson from the world of advertising. Look at the hard, creative work that advertising agencies put into researching and presenting an advertising program to a client. Then compare it with too many public relations presentations to top executives. Where are the opinion polls, the editorial analyses, the examples of competitors' actions, the clear and dramatic visuals? A presentation does not have to be fancy—and it should not be expensive. But it should be complete enough to back up your case, whether you are trying to sell a new media relations program or a new salary and recognition plan for employees. It must demonstrate a clear understanding of your organization's goals, both short and long term. It also can be helpful to presell your programs to others in the organization who will benefit from them. They then are likely to support you in their own interest. All too often public relations people are in the position of selling not only our programs but also the need for them. Make sure your priorities are the same as your top management's. Then work with others in your organization whose needs you are attempting to solve, and turn your recommendation into a joint solution.

In Bob Haldeman's book *The Ends of Power* there is a story about Henry Kissinger that symbolizes the multiple roles of the media relations professional. Haldeman was very protective of access to President Nixon, and this was a continuing area of conflict between himself and Kissinger. One day Kissinger came into Haldeman's office saying he had to see the president right away. Haldeman asked why, and Kissinger pointed to a stack of pictures he had in his arm. "It's a Cuban seaport, Haldeman," Kissinger said, "and these satellite photos show the Cubans are building soccer fields. I have to see the president now. Who's in there with him?" Apparently it was an important meeting on the economy, and Haldeman thought Kissinger had taken leave of his senses. "Are you going to burst into the Oval Office and interrupt a critical meeting to tell the president the Cubans are building soccer fields?" Haldeman asked, incredulously. "Of course I am," Kissinger answered, as patiently as he could. "These soccer fields could mean war. Cubans play baseball. Russians play soccer."[10]

We too must be able to distinguish between "baseball fields" and "soccer fields"—and then, once we have made the determination, to understand the difference and recommend appropriate action. Only then will we have completed the circle that is—or should be—our job description: To professionally work with the media to *tell* our organization's story, and to take advantage of our daily contacts with reporters by listening not only to what they are *asking* but also what they are *saying*. Whether you are from the school that believes the media leads public opinion or reflects it, the opportunities are the same: Reporters are a key window to the world's view of our organizations, our products and our people. Reflecting their interests, anticipating their concerns, adapting our media relations efforts and suggesting new courses of action as a result of their input—that is what makes us valuable to our companies and clients. That is also what makes us true media relations professionals.

We sometimes complain that we do not get enough respect within our organizations. But so many of us who aspire to greater recognition do not fulfill management expectations. Sometimes we are carried away more by mechanics and methodology than by substance and measurable results. We cannot afford to confuse motion with progress—nor to do well that which should not have been done at all. We cannot claim authority merely from our place on the organization chart. Rather, we must prove we have skills that make us a valued part of the management team by using those skills to anticipate and then solve the problems that keep our bosses and CEOs awake at night. Only then will we forge the close ties with our CEO and other decision makers in our organizations that are essential to accomplish our counseling role.

We live in an environment of such complexity that almost each activity we confront requires new thought and sensitivity in applying the old principles. We need to help our organizations and clients see the world through a wide-angle lens, so that even those things which are far away or off on the sidelines come into focus. We have a responsibility to assimilate, interpret and clarify information we gather from the media and our publics, and get it to the right person or group. We should be measured not only by the amount of news coverage we generate or number of briefing papers we prepare but also by our ability to mobilize the appropriate response within our organizations. We should ensure our companies and clients have long-range plans reflecting both economic and social objectives, just as we provide guidance and discipline for making better decisions today. We should take care that our plans are operating like an architect's drawing: Changes can be made and arrangements altered while the basic structure remains a strong, workable blueprint for action.

Beyond that, we should put the same effort into the long-term "storm warning" job as we do into the short-term activities. We must become, as management consultant Harry Levinson puts it, "organizational radar taking soundings and helping to steer rather than expecting to be piloted."[11] We must gain the confidence of the top management of our organization or client so that when we disagree with them they know it is *not* because we are argumentative or do not understand their goals but rather because we feel we would be abdicating our responsibility if we were to become "yes men" or remain silent while they launch an unguided missile. We must gain their confidence so that we earn the right to offer counsel by persuasion, negotiation or exhortation. The trick is to rock the boat without making everyone sink. Yet we must retain our humility. Our value lies not so much in our knowledge as in our sources of information and our ability to come up with questions that ensure thoughtful evaluation and reasonable answers by other experts in the organization.

At the time of Anwar Sadat's death, Henry Kissinger wrote a moving obituary for *Time* magazine in which he described the characteristics that propelled that Egyptian president to the center of the world's stage. He was writing about great leaders in a lofty context, of course. But the same qualities should be our ideal if we are to become effective organizational counselors: "The difference between great and ordinary leaders is rarely formal intellect but insight," Kissinger wrote. "The great man understands the essence of a problem; the ordinary leader grasps only the symptoms. The great man focuses on the relationship of events to each other; the ordinary leader sees only a series of seemingly disconnected events. The great man has a vision of the future that enables him to place obstacles into perspective; the ordinary leader turns pebbles in the road into boulders. . . . But a statesman must never be viewed as starry-eyed. He must have vision and depth; he must also translate his intuition into reality against sometimes resistant material."[12]

The environment in which our companies and clients operate is not one filled with easy managerial decisions to make in isolation or at a leisurely pace. The competitive marketplace has little tolerance for complacency. To succeed, our organizations must offer products and services that meet our customers' expressed needs—not our assumptions of those needs. As counselors, we should help our organizations manage the future by establishing programs that detect emerging public issues and demands early, analyze their ramifications, track and respond to them as they develop, evaluate the results, and modify activities based on this knowledge. We must demonstrate that we have a solid grasp of both our organization's objectives and the world in which we are operating, so that we can provide concrete assistance in articulating and dealing with the complex problems top management faces in relating to this ever-changing environment.

We should help our organizations view themselves in a larger context, ensuring they are not isolated from the mainstream of cultural, political, economic and social thought. We should not only react wisely to changing circumstances but also, when appropriate, help create them. We should embark on a continuing search for the tools and talents required to help our companies and our clients both deal with immediate issues and plan for future challenges. More important even than the technological revolution that is carrying us into the Information Age is the ever-changing socioeconomic scene in which our organizations operate. We would never let our executives walk into a news media interview without preparing them for tough questions we expected from the reporter. By the same token, we cannot let our organizations move unprepared into next year—or into the next decade.

NOTES

PREFACE

1. Alvin Toffler, *The Third Wave* (New York: William Morrow & Co., 1980), p. 183.
2. Quoted in Gloria Morris, "Market Opinion Research Gives the Competitive Edge," *Matrix*, Winter 1981, p. 19.
3. Dan Rather, "An Anchorman's Views of the News on Television," *Wall Street Journal*, 5 August 1982.
4. Robert MacNeil, *The Right Place at The Right Time*, (Boston: Little, Brown and Co., 1982), p. 129.
5. *UPI Reporter*, United Press International, New York, 23 April 1981.
6. "CBS Criticizes Documentary but Stands By It," *New York Times*, 16 July 1982.
7. Quoted in *Peter's Quotations: Ideas for Our Time*, ed. Dr. Laurence J. Peter (New York: William Morrow & Co., 1977) p. 125.

CHAPTER ONE

1. *Gang Box*, newsletter of Daniel Construction Company, Greenville, South Carolina, April 1982, p. 3.
2. *PR Reporter*, vol. 25, no. 24 (June 14, 1982); 1–2.

3. Eileen Prescott, "Behind the Camera on Morning TV," *Public Relations Journal*, November 1983, p. 17.

4. *The Business-Media Relationship, American Management Association Research Study*, (AMACOM, 1981), p. 38.

CHAPTER FOUR

1. John A. Meyers, "A Letter from the Publisher," *Time*, 14 November 1983.

2. John A. Meyers, "A Letter from the Publisher," *Time*, 17 May 1982.

3. Dennis Holder, "The Los Angeles Times Reaches for the Top," *Washington Journalism Review*, July/August 1982, p. 17.

4. William Safire, "On Language: Exit Haigspeak," *New York Times Magazine*, 11 July 1982.

5. Ian M. Ross, address delivered at the Defense Communications Agency's Annual Dining Out, Washington, D.C., October 17, 1981.

6. Quoted by Ken Roman and Joel Raphaelson, *How to Write Better*, Ogilvy & Mather Inc., 1978, p. 10.

7. *UPI Reporter*, United Press International, New York.

CHAPTER FIVE

1. Joseph Heller, *Good as Gold*, (New York: Pocket Books 1979), p. 77.

2. David Wallechinsky, Irving and Amy Wallace, *The Book of Lists* (New York: Bantam Books, 1977), p. 469.

3. John O'Toole, *The Trouble with Advertising . . .* (New York: Chelsea House, 1981), p. 112.

4. *PR Reporter*, 28 September 1981, p. 4.

5. Quoted by Eliot Frankel, "Learning to Conquer 'Mike' Fright," *Washington Journalism Review*, July/August 1982, p. 32.

6. Ibid, p. 33.

7. Frankel, p. 32.

8. Quoted in "Why TV Interview Training?", the Executive Television Workshop, New York.

9. The New York Times staff, *Churchill in Memoriam: His Life, His Death, His Wit and Wisdom*, (New York: Bantam Books, 1965), p. 160.

10. Cover story, *Time*, 30 August 1982, p. 74.

11. "How to Handle the Press," *Newsweek*, 19 April 1982, p. 90.

12. Quoted by Tom Friedman, "Why Western Electric Has to Hustle," *New York Times*, 17 January 1982, Business section, p. F1.

13. Quoted by Susan Astarita, "Handle the Press With Finesse," *Savvy*, June 1981, p. 58.

14. *Newsweek*, April 19, 1982, p. 90.

15. William Safire, *On Language* (New York: Time Books, 1981), p. 138.

16. Robert MacNeil, *The Right Place at The Right Time* (Boston: Little, Brown and Company, 1982), p. 10.

17. Bill Adler and Bill Adler Jr., "He Keeps His Wit About Him," *Parade* magazine, excerpted from "The Reagan Wit."

18. Sally Bedell, "Why TV News Can't Be a Complete View of the World," *New York Times*, 8 August 1982, Arts and Leisure section, p. 1.

19. *Newsweek*, April 19, 1982, p. 90.

20. "The Editor's Desk", *Fortune*, 14 November 1983, p. 4.

21. Dan Rather, "An Anchorman's View of the News on Television," 5 August 1982, *Wall Street Journal*.

22. *U.S. News and World Report*, 5 August, 1982, p. 46.

CHAPTER SIX

1. *Business and Finance*, Dublin, Ireland, 23 September 1982.

2. "Ethics in Public Relations," *Public Relations Journal*, December 1982.

3. Ivan Hill, "Compromise and Conviction—The Ethical Dilemma," speech delivered to the Associated General Contractors, Houston, Texas, 15 March, 1982.

4. Jeanne Mann, "Improving Relations with the Media: Two Views," *Business and the Media*, vol. 111, no. 2 (Summer 1981).

5. Ibid.

6. Betty Jan Stearns, "Honesty Promotes Good Media/Business Relations," *IABC News*, June 1981, p. 3.

7. *The Business-Media Relationship, An AMA Research Study*, (AMACOM, 1981), pp. 39, 43.

8. Foreign Press Center brochure, Washington, D.C., 83-220(27).

CHAPTER SEVEN

1. "A New Hospital for Berkeley,"Independent & Gazette, 21 April 1980.

2. "Herrick Hospital An Innovator in Health Care," *Oakland Post*, 1 May 1980.

3. AT&T press kit materials for the Aspen Winternational World Cup Races, February 28–March 6, 1983.

4. "United Way Bypasses Cultural Differences" and "Technology Extends United Way's Reach," *IABC Communications World*, August 1982, pp. 1, 3, 14.

5. "Westin Hotels: Anatomy of a Name Change," *Marketing Communications*, August 1982, p. 13.

6. "Attention to Detail Crucial in Event Promotions," *IABC Communications World,* July 1983, p. 1.

7. "Media Tactics Proposed to Reagan by Think Tank May Translate For Use by Practitioners & Their CEOs," *PR Reporter,* 27 April 1981, p. 1.

8. "Attention to Detail Crucial in Event Promotions," p. 9.

9. "Publisher's Memo," *Business Week,* 3 October 1983, p. 10.

CHAPTER EIGHT

1. Robert MacNeil, "The Right Place at The Right Time" (Boston: Little, Brown and Company, 1982), p. 89.

2. Letter to A. G. Hodges, April 4, 1864, "Life and Works of Abe Lincoln," Century Edition, Volume 8, (New York: Current Literature Publishing Co., 1907) p. 124.

3. "News Crews, Expecting the Worst, Prepare To Cover a Major Earthquake in California," *Wall Street Journal,* 24 June 1983, p. 25.

4. "Toxic-waste Scare 'Killed' Small Town, Its People Complain," *Wall Street Journal,* 1 March 1983, p. 1.

5. Ibid.

6. "Superfund's Cleansing Touch," *Fortune,* 20 September 1982, p. 60 and "Superfund, Supermess," *Time,* 21 February 1983, p. 14.

7. "Reagan Goal of Easing Environmental Laws is Largely Unattained," *Wall Street Journal,* 18 February 1983, p. 1.

8. "Western Conservation Drive Cuts Light Bill By $91,000," Gainesville, Georgia, *Times,* 12 October 1980.

9. "Recycling Plastic Trash into Treasure," *Design News,* 19 October 1981, p. 14.

10. *Telephony,* 7 September 1981.

11. "Raking It In," *Lexington* (Kentucky) *Leader,* 31 August 1981.

12. "Raking It In for Reuse," *Phoenix Gazette,* 5 August 1981.

13. "Don Procknow On: Energy Conservation As Corporate Policy," *Electronic Engineering Times,* Speakout Series, June 1981, p. 3.

14. Ongoing coverage in *The Journal,* West Columbia, S.C., *The Record,* Columbia, S.C., and *The Dispatch News,* Lexington, S.C. from March 17 to April 28, 1982.

15. *Seattle Post–Intelligencer,* 15 March 1982, p. 1.

16. *American Banker,* 23 March 1982.

17. *Seattle Post–Intelligencer,* 31 March 1982, p. A9.

18. *Seattle Post–Intelligencer,* 31 March 1982, p. A12.

19. Ibid.

20. Talk by D. L. Hilder, "Recent Trend Is in Human Resources and Labor Relations," 1980 Public Relations Conference, Princeton, N.J., October 9, 1980.

21. "1.5 Million May Feel Sexually Harassed, Study Says," *Globe and Mail,* 6 April 1983, p. 1.

22. Quoted by Lucille deView in a review of "Writing Without Bias," *Media Reporter*, Brennam Publications, England.

23. Quoted in the Baltimore *News American*, June 25, 1980, p. 11-A.

24. James Wolcott, "Son of Kong," *New York*, 11 October 1982, p. 80.

25. "Crisis Plans Tested in KC Hyatt Hotel Disaster," IABC *Communications Journal*, August 1981, p. 1.

26. "Robberies Help Inspire Bank's Crisis PR Plan," IABC *Communications Journal*, June 1982, p. 8.

27. Dan Cordtz, "Why Business Won't Talk," *Business and the Media*, The Media Institute, Fall 1980.

28. Quoted in "Business Says Product Recall Makes Sense," *New York Times*, 17 October 1981, p. 9.

29. Quoted in "Handle the Press With Finesse," *Savvy*, June 1981, p. 57.

30. Quoted in "Johnson & Johnson Officials Take Steps To End More Killings Linked to Tylenol," *Wall Street Journal*, October 4, 1982, p. 16.

31. Quoted in "Tylenol's 'Miracle' Comeback," *Time*, 17 October 1983, p. 67.

32. Quoted in "Solid Consumer Relations Can Defuse Crisis," *Public Relations Journal*, December 1982, p. 8.

CHAPTER TEN

1. Alexander Kendrick, *Prime Time*, (Boston-Toronto: Little Brown and Co. 1969), p. 456.

2. Steven E. Goodman, "Why Few Corporations Monitor Social Issues," *Public Relations Journal*, April 1983, p. 20.

3. Carl Sagan, "A Gift in Vividness," *Time*, 20 October 1980, p. 68.

4. "Congressional Anger on Free Trade Could Lead to Some Major Changes," *Wall Street Journal*, 17 March 1983, p. 30.

5. "Public Perceptions of Restructuring: An Overview," Summary of AT&T-sponsored research efforts in 1982.

6. Donald E. Procknow, speech delivered to AT&T Western Electric Public Relations managers, Princeton, N.J., October 15, 1982.

7. "Communication Plays Key Role, Say Hospital CEOs", IABC *Communications Journal*, April 1981, p. 7.

8. Charles Marshall, speech delivered at AT&T Public Relations Vice Presidents Conference, West Palm Beach, Florida, March 15, 1983.

9. John J. Pappas, talk to Teletype Corporation Integrated Promotions Task Force, Skokie, Illinois, August 3, 1981.

10. H. R. Haldeman and Joseph DiMona, *The Ends of Power*, (New York: Times Books, 1978), p. 85.

11. Harry Levinson, lecture delivered to AT&T–Pace University Executive Management Program, New York City.

12. Henry A. Kissinger, "A Man with a Passion for Peace," *Time*, 19 October 1981, p. 12.

BIBLIOGRAPHY

AMACOM. *The Business-Media Relationship, An AMA Research Study,*
1981.
AT&T. *PR Indicators,* A Quarterly Summary of Data on Bell System Public
Relations Departments. 1981.
Chapman, Ray. "Measurement: It Is Alive and Well in Chicago." *Public
Relations Journal* (May 1982): 28–29.
Chesapeake and Potomac Telephone Companies. *Making Media Relations
Work, A Guide for C & P News Contact People.* Washington, D.C.
Editor & Publisher. "Business News Releases Faulted in Editor Survey."
(6 June 1981):86.
Getting Yourself Known in the Community. New York: Anderson Press.
1981.
Honaker, Charles. "News Releases Revisited." *Public Relations Journal*
(April 1981):25–27.
Hunter, William. "Progress Showing in Business/Media Battle." *IABC News*
(June 1981):9.
Moskal, Brian. "Why Companies Avoid the Limelight." *Industry Week* (21
July 1980): 53–57.
The National Center for Business and Economic Communication. *The
American University Newsletter:* 11:9. (1 May, 1982).
Ricklefs Roger, "Despite Some Gripes, Bosses Say Business Press Is Gen-
erally Good." *Wall Street Journal,* 21 September 1982.
Rossie, Chuck. "Writing News Releases: Some Free Advice." *The Journalist*
(Fall 1983):16.

Stevenson, H. L. *UPI Reporter*, newsletter, 23 April 1981.

Wann, Al. Media Relations Workshop conducted at annual conference of International Association of Business Communications. Chicago. 1982.

Weber, Samuel. "A Basic Training Document: What the Press Feels We Should Know About Working with the Press. *Tips and Tactics*, a supplement of *PR Reporter* 19:13 (22 June 1981).

Western Electric. *Media Relations, A Guide for Western Electric Spokespersons.* May 1980.

Yale, David. "External Relations Require Careful Planning." *IABC News* (November 1981): 11.

Yale, David R. *The Publicity Handbook.* New York: Bantam Books. 1982.

INDEX